JAMES M

The Magic of Method Selling

Revolutionary New Sales Ideas, Based on Old World Truth

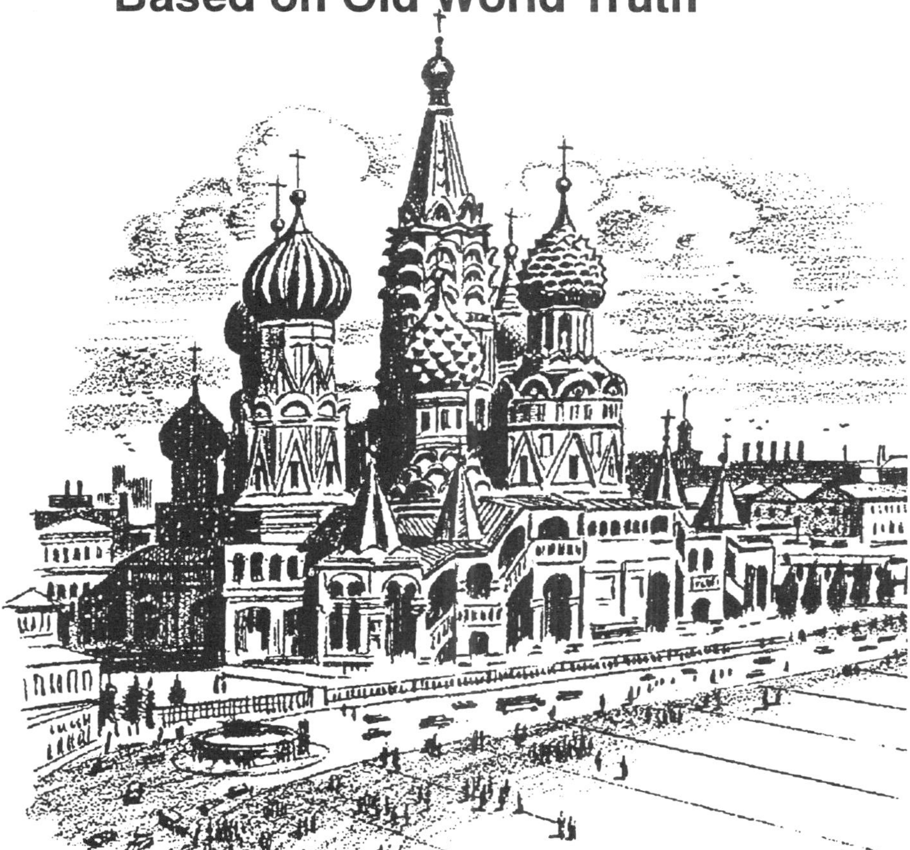

A Cut to the Chase Publication

Library of Congress Catalog Card Number:
ISBN#: 0-9641729-0-9

ACKNOWLEDGEMENTS

Special thanks to my drama professor at Southwest Texas University, Jim Harrell. He introduced me to Stanislavski at the young age of 19. Jim is a lesson in perseverance. You may have seen him in small bit parts in such movies as J.F.K., Paper Moon, Jaws, and Urban Cowboy.
A sincere appreciation to Robert L. Moody, Chairman of the Board of American National Insurance Company and National Western Life, for his belief in me.

I want to thank Sonia Moore for her insights, and passion for her teacher and mentor, Constantin Stanislavski.

To my mother, Sharon, for her unconditional love and confidence in me.

A special thanks to Tammy Wood for her diligent, dedicated work on the typing of the manuscript, and to Rita Keller for the editing on this project.

Tremendous gratitude to the thousands of people who trusted me to invest in a product through my associates and myself. A big thanks to you for sharing this time with me, and it is my sincere desire that the knowledge you gain from this book will outweigh the time and the resources you have invested.

Remember, just one idea can dramatically change and improve your sales performance.

Wishing you the very best.

TABLE OF CONTENTS

Preface

Method Selling

In the myriad of books and tapes on sales and management training, there emerges a common theme comprised of techniques and cute phrases to be used on people. This book approaches the subject from a uniquely different perspective. Let's put a human face on sales professionals, and direct our attention to the human side of sales training. There are some fundamental questions we need to address:

> Why is there such a high turnover in the sales profession?
> What impact does sales management play in this alarming statistic?
> Is there a system which can improve the success of sales professionals and build strong cohesive teams of quality individuals?

First of all, only a very small minority of people enter the sales profession as their first choice. Many individuals begin a second career in sales for a variety of reasons stemming from a need for additional income, to rebounding from a disappointment in another endeavor. Unfortunately, there are many people who apply for sales jobs with the attitude that they will do this until something better comes along. The automobile industry is an excellent example. Think for a moment of how many cars you have purchased in your lifetime. How many car salesmen called you back to purchase a new model? Do you think the 90% turnover rate in the industry would have something to do with this situation?

Sales is a critical function for most companies, yet many managers' strategy is to throw 100 sales reps against the wall, hoping ten will stick. Hiring and training sales representatives is an expensive activity, not to mention the fact that these sales reps become your company in the eyes of the public.

Method Selling is a system which can provide "method to the madness" of training sales representatives. This book provides the path for the sales representative to follow in the quest to becoming a top flight sales professional. Method Selling provides a refreshing new approach to the role of the sales professional by incorporating Stanislavski's teaching of "Method Acting." The insights into the execution of the performance of the presentation ensures professionalism and results. The productivity of the entire sales team will improve with the knowledge of the sales process.

Everyone who owns or manages a company knows the importance of an effective sales team. It is everyone's objective to be successful. However, we often focus on succeeding without developing a true understanding of the components of success. We see only the end result of what we are hoping to accomplish. As we read about the successes of companies and individuals, we discover their successes were rooted in preparation, proper planning, and positive activity. What determines activity? Feelings and purpose are the pillars for positive constructive activity. You could compare feelings and purpose to a sailboat. Feelings would represent the sails and purpose would be the rudder. I love the old saying which states, "If you can't change the wind, change the direction of your sails." Controlling your feelings is important in the emotional climate of your world.

Going deeper and deeper into the process, you will find thoughts. Thoughts are the most powerful force in the world today. Thoughts can be creative or destructive depending on the user of this power. Thoughts are magnetic in nature and will draw to you what you desire or what you fear. What determines your thoughts? The answer is ideas. Ideas can enlighten and enrich your life and those around you. Method Selling is a collection of ideas designed to improve productivity of sales professionals. Many of the ideas will gently nudge your memory banks. You will find other truths which could dramatically change your view of the role you play in your career.

For some of you who are entering the sales field for the first time, Method Selling will provide solid informative data to educate you on the basics of selling, For the old sales pros, Method Selling provides a unique opportunity to enhance your talent in effectively executing your sales presentation. You will be able to incorporate many of the concepts into your daily interactions with your clients and prospects. It might just get you re-energized about the challenging rewarding position you now possess.

Method Selling is your resource for ideas. If you are open and receptive, these ideas will become part of your thought processes. These thoughts will generate feelings, which lead to your purpose. When feelings and purpose unite you have set your course for positive constructive activity. When you execute your actions with the information you gain from Method Selling, you will discover on the horizon Success, Your Success.

Publisher Note

We are pleased to bring you, *The Magic of Method Selling*, which outlines a proven path for you to chart your course for success in selling. As you read and re-read this unique book, you will find between the covers a special message which will enhance your sales performance and the quality of your life. Method Selling will become your reference guide, which you can refer to time and again for information which will improve your effectiveness as a sales professional.

We are so confident you will improve your sales performance we are offering a complete money back guarantee. We would like to hear from you about your improvement and success, so please take just a few minutes and fill out our short questionnaire. We will send you a special gift upon receipt of your form. If you would like to share *The Magic of Method Selling* with others, I have enclosed an order form with volume discounts for orders of fifty or more copies. Thank you for your interest in this innovative new approach to sales training. Best of luck in your sales and personal life.

Introduction

"From the very beginning, the Stanislavski system ranked the problems of acting with a knowledge of human psychology"

- Nikolai A. Gorchakov

Method Selling is an exciting new way to develop skill and understanding in the area of selling. Although Method Selling is a new concept in the training of sales professionals, the undercurrent is based on elements designed by a Russian actor/director named Constantin Stanislavski in the early 1900's. The elements continue to evolve and expand in the modern age. Stanislavski taught his actors the techniques that he felt would make them more effective actors. His system has been called "Method Acting" by the experts in the field of drama. It is my strong belief that Stanislavski's work in the development of his system will benefit the sales performance of all individuals who seek to study and absorb and apply the ideas presented in this book.

Before the era of *glasnost,* the former Soviet Union had allowed one valuable commodity to be exported to the world. This commodity, however, was confined to the artistic community. It was not the teachings of Karl Marx, it was the wisdom of Stanislavski.

Every country has rare treasures that unite its people and create a sense of nationalism. A treasure that is, in essence, theirs to be cherished and nurtured. Russia takes pride in its art, which is full of color, beauty and tradition. Stanislavski developed a system that changed the Soviet's theater art forever and launched it to higher levels of performance and quality.

The exciting news for us is that the principles of this system can be transferred into the area of salesmanship. "What?" you may say. "Selling is not theater!" Selling is an art, a wonderful and exciting art. Method Selling is a system that can transform ordinary salespeople into superstars in their profession. A system that can take that boring, worn presentation that has been made so many times, that has lost the meaning of its original purpose, and breathe new life into it. The discovery of this system came about in my search for meaning in the area of sales training.

There are many schools of thought for successful selling. Unfortunately, the literature all seems to describe techniques and superficial words used to manipulate a prospect into buying. The hundreds of books and tapes on selling only begin to scratch the surface of what I believe true selling is all about. Companies spend thousands of dollars on extravagant pamphlets and sales materials, and forget about the most important part of the sales equation - the salesperson. Consequently, they spend very little on the development of the salesperson.

It is time to take a deep look into our lives and find the true motivation toward our objective, not only in our careers, but in our own very existence. The magic word in life is hope. Hope for the big sale, hope for the promotion, hope for a better life. There is gold in these pages, which I truly hope you will absorb.

The ironic part of this whole project is that I have used concepts and principles designed by a man from a former communist country to show how you can increase your own personal wealth and perpetuate one of the most precious gems of our society, capitalism. Salesmanship personifies capitalism. A man or woman with little or no education, and without the benefit of a wealthy family, can obtain wealth, even enormous wealth, by mastering the art of selling.

The premise behind the Method Selling concept is that effective sales professionals and talented high income actors share many commonalities. They are both dedicated to their professions and they are master communicators. The actor communicates with fellow actors and the audience. The master sales person communicates with prospects. In interviews with actors and top notch sales professionals, they both express a true love for their work. Actors who enjoy their roles find the movie or play is completed and they have to look for their next role. The tremendous advantage that you have as a sales professional is that you have more control of your income and your career. You also determine how many times you perform your presentation. Both groups perform their roles, which include dialog, movement, and should contain emotion that will move the audience. I see a real need to train sales professionals much like actors are trained in the theater. One of the most respected training program for actors comes from the Soviet Union.

The concepts of method acting were designed by the master director/actor, Constantin Stanislavski, from Russia. Learning Method Selling requires discipline and practice in order to understand the teachings of Stanislavski. Studying these techniques, you will learn the basics of the system, as well as the process of the sale and many other insights which will assist you in your role as a sales professional. This project will provide you the foundation to build into your presentation dynamic, revolutionary truths which will completely change your approach to your selling career.

Method Selling will enhance and sharpen your performance in the theater of selling.

Method Selling

"A New Beginning"

"Method Selling is not mere window dressing, it is a system which will guide you in your quest to become a high performing professional sales person."

- JMR

As you embark on your journey through the principles of Method Selling, it is important that you approach the work with an open mind. For you see, the mind that criticizes or is judgmental is not the same mind that can absorb, learn, and appreciate the material presented. Anytime you are exposed to new ideas, there is a natural tendency to resist the concepts. To maximize the benefits of Method Selling, it is advisable to practice the principles presented in the text.

The key to learning fresh new ideas is to associate these ideas with something you are already familiar with in your life. A living example took place at a recent workshop that I was involved with last month. One of the individuals wanted to discuss a project with me after the meeting. She told me to call her. She told me her room number was 1620; however I didn't have a pen handy, so I associated the numbers with sweet 16 and my old football number 20. Later that evening the numbers came to me as naturally as the sunrise in the east. The purpose of this story is to illustrate that you will be learning powerful ways to improve your sales performance, yet many of the ideas are those you may have learned in your third grade school play. Remember when you had to be someone different. In fact, you may have had to be an inanimate object, such as a tree. The teachers made it easier for you when they dressed you up with leaves and a trunk. They also gave you instructions on just how a tree is to be portrayed in a play. A demonstration from the instructor gave you the needed insight into your role as a tree.

Method Selling is not mere window dressing; it is a system which will guide you in your quest to become a high performing professional sales person. As you build your blueprint for your sales career, or are fine-tuning it, a foundation is needed. Method Selling is unique in the training of sales people, yet before we discuss, analyze, and utilize the concepts, let us first study the word, Method.

Everywhere you turn, everyone seems to be using acronyms to share information with others. Acronyms help you assimilate the ideas into your life. The acronym, METHOD, will help you mentally prepare for this innovative, new approach to selling that is based on old world truths from the mind of Constantin Stanislavski.

Management

Management has been defined as the art of getting objectives and goals accomplished through others, helping them to do what they know they should do, but doing it in a way that they feel they want to do it. You should keep in mind that, although you may have a manager, you are the manager of your life. You oversee many different departments in your life. First of all, you are in charge of the career department. You decided which industry you would affiliate with and the type of work you would do. In life, you are very fortunate to have selected the greatest business in the world, selling. Second, you are the manager of your time. You are the boss of how you spend the 1,440 minutes of your day. The best insight into time management is the approach that there are three major blocks of time: eight hours for work, eight hours for sleeping and daily upkeep, and eight hours that are described as discretionary. You determine how you spend these hours. You can clearly see how much control you possess in your life.

This was illustrated to me during a visit to a large insurance company, where I noticed an interesting sign that a secretary had on her wall; it was entitled, "So You Want a Day Off," and reads, "Let's take a look at what you are asking for. There are 365 days per year available for work, and you already have two days off per week, leaving you 261 days available for work; since you spend 16 hours each day away from work, you have used up 170 days, leaving only 91 days available. You spend 30 minutes each day on your coffee break. That accounts for 23 days each year, leaving only 68 days available. With a one hour lunch period each day, you have used up another 26 days, leaving only 22 days available for work. You normally spend two days per year on sick leave. This leaves you only 20 days available for work. We are off for five holidays per year, so your available working time is down to 15 days. We generously give you 14 days vacation per year which leaves only one day available for work, and I'll be damned if you are going to take that day off."

Stress management is another department that deserves your attention. The stress factor didn't even exist on an intellectual level when my grandfather was hitting the pavement; it has now become a science among psychologists and seminar leaders. This is an area where you can exercise your authority. Remember, it is not what happens to you; it is how you react to the events in your life that matters. Stress is a natural part of living, yet stress can be positive or negative, once again depending on you.

Stress in a positive form can be described as excitement, however, in a negative form it can destroy your physical, emotional, and mental life. Stress can creep into your life as a lion stalks its prey; you feel the symptoms but are not consciously aware of its presence. The next thing you know you are in a situation when you feel, on a sub-conscious level, that you are in danger and there is no way out. The famous "flight or fight" attempts to go into effect and you can't respond. You are literally stuck. **You are a self manager**. Recognize those conditions and plan to overcome them. When you start to feel yourself filling your head with stressful thoughts, stop and replace those thoughts with positive and peaceful ones. You already know this, but why don't you do it? Be good to yourself, because you work for you.

The next department is physical apparatus. This department falls under your job requirements. Take a long look at yourself; if by chance you had another person in charge of this department, would he or she receive a bonus or risk losing his or her job. Your physical body tells a lot about you. With the exception of bone structure, you do control to a great degree how you look to others. We all do not have to look like a Julia Roberts or Tom Cruise, but if there are improvements to be made, you are the only one authorized to implement the changes. Words of warning: don't let the scales run your life, and throw away those weight tables. Everyone wears weight differently, so find the weight you feel comfortable in. The physical fitness department must not be neglected. Regular exercise will keep you fit and will relieve stress. The nutritional department also falls under your domain. What goes into your body is your responsibility. The attitude department sets in motion the atmosphere for the entire organization. There are many other departments in your life, but the point here is that you are the manager, you are the boss, you control your fate.

Expectancy

In most cases you get what you expect. Expectancy is an important part of Method Selling for the simple reason that what you expect to obtain from this book will be a self-fulfilling prophecy. This same truth applies in your life. Make it a point to ingrain in your mind that **failure is impossible**. Expect the best from life. The Optimist International Creed contains a powerful reference to expectancy; it states "To think only of the best, to work only for the best, and to expect only the best." Expectancy puts a spring in your step and gives you that extra something that separates winners from losers. In the *Dynamics of Personal Goal Setting*, produced by Success Motivation Institute, Paul J. Meyer writes, "As you begin to experience the fulfillment of your expectations and to realize that you are indeed becoming what you prophesied, belief in your own potential to succeed increases rapidly. Your expectations grow and expand to include new versions of what you can do, and what you can become." Greet each new day with a surge of strength that comes from your expectancy.

Training

Mark Twain wrote, "Training is everything." Those words are profound. Training will dictate your sales performance, your sales results, and success in your career. An old coach of mine preached that practice doesn't always improve performance, but perfect practice will, every time. It is essential for you to put into perfect practice concepts that you will discover between the covers of this book. Training takes place in the office as you interact with your peers. It takes place in the offices of your prospects. Training also takes place during the quiet moments at home or on your walks in the evening.

Listen to the voice that constantly lectures you. What is it telling you? Does it say that you are a winner, that you have unlimited opportunity for wealth and peace-of-mind, or does it tell you that you are just not good enough, that you don't quite measure up, or that you just don't have what it takes to get the job done. Your best trainer is you, and the voice you hear is your voice. As in the theater, the production's success is rooted in the director, the playwright and the talent of the actors. There are countless hours for rehearsal, planning, exercises, and then more rehearsals for the four to 14 days of a theatrical production. How much time do we practice on the production that we perform our entire careers? Do you have a sales script? Have you studied the script? Do you have a full understanding of the objectives of the presentation? Have you memorized the words and the meaning behind the words? Am I advocating a canned sales presentation? Think about specialists in the medical field; they follow the same procedures, day after day, for their operations. It is important that you have guidelines to follow in every face-to-face interview and questions to ask that qualify the prospect.

Training also occurs in actual sales presentations. That is why you need to have as many presentations as you can schedule. When you are selling, you are earning income, or you are in the process of getting better through training.

Homeostasis

Homeostasis is the desire to stay the same, to go along, to stop at the status quo. It is a condition that affects millions of people, and it is a major obstacle in your development. Homeostasis not only blocks individual growth, but can affect entire corporations. It prompts you to resist incorporating new ideas. The destination of the person who has acquired this ailment is referred to as the "comfort zone." When sales professionals check into this zone, they ride on past successes, and cease doing those important activities that got them to that point in their careers. This may sound unusual, but success in sales can breed failure in sales, if you get caught in the trap of complacency. How do you know when you are breaking out of your homeostasis? You feel it when you start to get nervous, or you feel uncomfortable in life's situations. So it is important to overcome your homeostasis; realizing that everything in life is changing every day. In fact, you have heard it said that the only thing in life that doesn't change is change itself. Did you know that every cell in your body is reproduced every seven years? In the business culture, everything changes, including your markets, your products, and your customers. So homeostasis should not be part of your personality.

How do you step out of the darkness and into the sunlight of growth and prosperity? First of all, don't be afraid to try new ideas; the more you try new material, the easier it will be for you. Practice your new behavior, prior to opening night. Visualize the end result of the new idea, and you will find that you will feel in total control of your world. The fact that you are reading this book is a very positive step toward becoming the person you will ultimately become in the future. Remember the four A's in your battles with homeostasis. First of all, **Assess** your current situation. Ask yourself, what new ideas have you learned this year? Are you keeping up with the changes in your company, industry, and clients' needs? Secondly, **Accept** the humbling fact that you can never learn everything there is to know about anything, yet that doesn't mean that you should become complacent. What it does mean is that you can become proficient in your field, and that there will always be new ideas and procedures that you need to learn in your profession. Next is the art of **Assimilating** the new information into your presence, presentation, and personality. The last step is to **Affirm** that you are committed to discovering all of the bright opportunities that this world has to offer.

Optimum Performance

When you learn, experience and integrate the Method Selling concepts, you will be armed and ready to reach optimum performance. Have you ever experienced optimum performance, when everything was on the mark, and you felt confident and in control? Communication was open between you and your prospect. You had adequate time to perform your presentation.

Your prospect was a qualified candidate who needed and wanted the products you had to offer. How did you feel? What did optimal performance look like? Optimum performance should be the goal of every sales professional. When you made a sale, did you ever stop and analyze why you were successful? On the other hand, when things were not accomplished in the presentation, do you know why? It is important after every single presentation to replay all of the events, taking notes as the show is unveiled. Optimum performance shouldn't be an occasional happening; rather it should be preplanned and executed on a daily basis. When you are in optimum performance, it is actually easier and more fun than the old way of doing business. Apply the principles of Method Selling to arrive at your optimum performance level.

Development

Development is the emergence of the dormant potential within yourself. I like to think of development as the retention and application of knowledge. Knowledge is found in the seeds of learning. Learning is made up of four stages.

The first stage is *unconsciously incompetent*. This is when you don't even know that you don't know how to do something.

The second stage is *consciously incompetent.* Reality sets in and you realize that you don't have the experience or the education to do the task.

The third level is *consciously competent*. You start to develop and are aware that you can accomplish the objectives. You suddenly understand that you know the job or task.

The last stage of learning is when you become *unconsciously competent*. This is when you do the right things naturally without conscious thought. Stanislavski said, "In the first period of conscious work in a role, an actor feels his way into the life of his part, without altogether understanding what is going on in it, in him and around him."

Stanislavski believed in the development and the conditioning of the mind when he wrote, "When he reaches the region of the subconscious the eyes of the soul are opened and he is aware of everything, every minute detail, and it acquires an entirely new significance."

Stanislavski, the Man

1863-1938

It is important to first give background information on Constantin Stanislavski. Mr. Stanislavski was a talented actor and director in the Soviet Union. Stanislavski was born Constantin Alekseieva on the fifth day of January, 1863, to the proud parents of Vladimir and Elizaveta Alekseieva of Russia. He later changed his name to Stanislavski. Stanislavski was one of 10 children and was fortunate to be brought up in an environment of wealth and culture. His family owned a textile business.

During the mid 1800's, Russia was in a period of transformation in its artistic identity. Stanislavski's family status in the community and the influence of his parents gave him access to the creative arts. He was educated at home, where he studied mathematics, grammar, and French. His father stressed physical fitness, and part of Stanislavski's physical education included dance and a full gymnasium in which to practice.

He was not an outstanding student and was a sickly child. To overcome his fears, Stanislavski learned to use his imagination. The children in the family all played out scenes from plays to entertain the family. As a boy, he was fascinated by the theater, which provided him the excitement that the ordinary classroom did not provide. His father purchased a building that contained a smaller building, which was converted into a small theater. Stanislavski participated in the amateur productions where he perfected his craft as an actor.

He was greatly influenced by the Mali Theater known as the home of "Psychological Realism." Stanislavski's cousin Nikolin, mayor of Moscow, appointed him chairman of the Russian music society in 1886. This appointment led to his influence within the artistic community. Stanislavski made his directing debut with the production of Moliere's *Le Marriage Force* in 1882. He appeared in many amateur productions.

Stanislavski wanted to start a school to train actors in theater arts. As early as 1885, he began to organize acting principles inspired by the writings of Nikolai Struzhkin. In the late 1880's he started the Moscow Amateur Music Dance Circle. One of his biggest accomplishments was the founding of the Moscow Art Theatre which served as Stanislavski's laboratory in his experiments to uncover the secret to effective acting. He went on to produce many professional plays such as *The Three Sisters*, *The Cherry Orchard* and *The Seagull*. He dedicated his life, searching for a training system for actors. His work encompassed over fifty years of acting, directing, and teaching in the theater.

He, like so many of us, stopped one day and asked himself an ever important question, "Where has the joy gone in my work?" Stanislavski believed that a role and art can never become tiring. Yet, if we are to take the attitude that we are playing a role as a sales person, and that selling is an art, then why do we become tired and burned out with the profession?

Stanislavski discovered that the more he repeated his roles the more he slipped into a stale stage. He said, "Examining my past step by step, I came to see clearer and clearer that the inner content which was put into a role during its first creation and the inner content that was born in my soul with the passing of time were as far apart as the heaven and the earth." Too many times sales people also slip into a sort of "automatic pilot" role. They are not fully conscious of what they say or do; they just go through the motion of selling. Stanislavski realized that same weakness in the actors he worked with who fell into that trap. He set out to discover a system that would awaken the creativity and the spontaneity of his actors, through physical action and to create performances that were true to life works of art. There are many interpretations of his work which vary from one extreme to the other.

Method Selling relates the principles of the system he used to deal with actors, and relates it to the art of selling, thereby creating sales presentations that are true to life, and will also be works of art.

Method Selling
The Power System

"If you are not reaching a certain point and need a different choice to get there, then you need the Method."

- Kim Hunter

The Method Selling Training System is a revolutionary new way to train yourself to be a high performance sales professional, using the teachings of one of the world's most respected directors in the creative arts industry. Through years of study, Stanislavski discovered the path to one's own creative state. The western world has a tendency to break things down to study the individual parts. However, with the Stanislavski teaching and the Method Selling training program, we must view the concept as a whole. You see that in order for you to reach the peak performance you seek, the total concept of Method Selling must be incorporated. It is my attempt to share with you the concept as Stanislavski would have wanted it expressed truthfully, logically, and most importantly, enthusiastically. In the research, it is amazing to see his work adapt and change from one project to another.

Discover Your Potential Selling Talent

Method Selling is an alternative way to study the art of selling. There are many factors that contribute to the dynamics of the system.

It is important to first understand the system. Method Selling is both a science and an art. It is a science because it is based on Stanislavski's experiments and his unique discoveries. It is an art when you put the system into action with your sales performance. It has been called the science of theater art. The beauty of the system is that it is continually growing and changing.

The system gives you the option of discovering your potential selling talent by targeting guidelines for you in the area of realism. In fact, Stanislavski could have been called "The Father of Realism" for his quest in presenting truthful and realistic acting to the people of Russia.

It has been said that art is an imitation of life. In Russia, in the late 1800's, the popular theme for the Russian theater was the staging and posing style of acting. Stanislavski felt that if he could discover the natural creative mood, then he could create performances that were true to life and, more importantly, believable to the audience.

Stanislavski wrote, "The solution of this problem had become the regular enthusiasm of Stanislavski: as my friends expressed themselves. There was nothing that I left undone in order to solve the mystery. I watched myself closely, I looked into my soul, so to say, on the stage and off. I watched other men and actors, when I rehearsed my new parts or their new parts with them. I also watched them from the auditorium. I performed all sorts of experiments with them and myself. I tortured them; they grew angry and said that actors were not guinea pigs to be used for experimentation. And they were right in their protest."

Stanislavski, early in his development of the system, directed the actors' responsibility into six basic elements, which we will use as a guide to developing your role as a sales professional. Adapting the process to your sales career, you would begin with:

wanting - your desire to enter the field of selling and start earning income
seeking - your desire is a catalyst to search for the needed material to become a top performing sales person; this includes your inter-personal traits and physical things such as clothes, car, and sales material.
experiencing - you create and visualize the inner and outer role you want to embrace.
impersonating - you start to act as if you are that role.
blending - the merging of experience and impersonation takes place.
influencing - the presentation comes to life, thereby allowing the prospect to share your inner world.

Stanislavski pursued his search for realism in acting as a scientist searches for a cure for a disease. Lee Strasberg had this to say about Stanislavski's system, "The important thing in the Stanislavski method is that it is the opposite of a system. A system implies a theory with precise rules of what to do exactly at each moment. Systems of the past were exactly that. You had specific ways of doing things in different situations. The Stanislavski method is no system. It does not deal with the results to be attained and therefore sets no rules for what should be done. It only tries to show the actor the path to be followed, how he goes about finding what only he can find and what, even when he has found it, cannot be repeated the next time, but must be the next time found again."

Earlier, I mentioned that Stanislavski came from a former communist country, yet his principles are universal and transcend political thought. His teachings have helped thousands of actors improve the truthfulness of their performance and elevated their talent to new heights. Those very principles are available to you and will help in achieving a greater degree of success in your sales career.

Why doesn't Russia use the Stanislavski System to improve its economy and make its motherland more self reliant? The answer lies in the economic system that the Russians had incorporated. Let us take just a few minutes to discuss the difference as it relates to the selling profession. When Russia was a communist country, it didn't have a need for sales people. The country's supply of virtually everything dealing with the consumer market was limited. The equation for supply side economics is supply and demand. When a country has limited supplies, it doesn't want to stimulate demand. In contrast, in the United States there is an abundant supply, so it is important that we continue to have the demand to distribute the product or service to the consumer.

Ayn Rand wrote a beautiful book entitled *Capitalism: The Unknown Ideal.* In her book she discussed many aspects pertaining to capitalism. She wrote, "There are only two fundamental questions or two aspects of the same question that determine the nature of any social system; does a social system recognize individual rights? And, does a social system ban physical force from human relationships?

The answer to the second question is the practical implementation of the answer to the first."

It is not the intent of this book to initiate a political debate. However, it is important to know that our jobs as sales people are based on the capitalistic system. As long as the system survives, you will never be without a job. Yes, some companies do lay off sales people, and yes, some businesses will close their doors. However, the profession of selling will always be needed in a free enterprise system. Ayn Rand continues her thought on capitalism, "Is man a sovereign individual who owns his person, his mind, his life, his work and its products - or is he the property of the tribe (the state, the society, the collective) that may dispose of him in any way it pleases, that may dictate his convictions, prescribe the course of his life, control his work and expropriate his products? Does man have the right to exist for his own sake - or is he born in bondage, as an indentured servant who must acquire it free and clear? This is the first question to answer. The rest is consequences and practical implications. The basic issue is only: Is man free? In mankind's history, capitalism is the only system that answers: Yes."

We all must be thankful for all the hard work and dedication that our founding fathers invested to create the system from which we derive our livelihood. You are free to grow to the heights you set for yourself.

Capitalism 101

"Led by an invisible hand to promote an end which was not part of his intention by pursuing his own interest, he frequently promotes that of the society more effectually than when he really intended to promote it."

- Adam Smith

Let's take a quick lesson on the subject of capitalism. As a sales professional, you are free to earn as much wealth as you want. You are free to choose the lifestyle you want to live. You are free to travel anywhere you want. You are free. Selling will allow you to realize the freedom that you have been given. It will do it at an accelerated pace when you master the art of Method Selling. Your job is made possible by our economic system.

The term "capitalism" was actually coined by Karl Marx in his writing describing the industrial nations. Capitalism is the heart of a free enterprise system. Capitalism, as the name implies, refers to capital, usually meaning money. However, capital may be found in other forms, such as stocks and bonds, commodities, etc. *Webster's New World Dictionary* defines capitalism as:

1. "A system under which the means of production, distribution, and exchanges in large measure are privately owned and directed."

2. "The concentration of capital in the hands of a few, or the resulting power or influence."
   And finally:

3. "A system favoring such concentration of wealth."

I consider these to be very narrow views of what capitalism is all about. Yet, there is an anti-capitalistic mentality in the United States of America. The very freedom that men gave their lives for more than 200 years ago is being used to undermine the foundation on which democracy was built. A prominent representative of big business said, "The people, at large, were apathetic and complacent...too busy playing golf, or looking at television, or tending to their businesses to protect the freedom and opportunity which have made America what it is."

That is a frightening picture of what America is becoming. The truth is, that was said in a 1949 meeting of the National Association of Manufacturers documented by Mr. Galbraith in his book, *American Capitalism*.

Bob L. Heilbroner, in his publication *The Limits of American Capitalism*, wrote, "In a fundamental sense, communism puts capitalism on trial before the bar of history - not with the advantages of a new society claiming the future, but with the disadvantages of an old society hanging onto the past. In this trial it matters not that communism has its own system of privilege, in some ways as primitive as our own. Nor does it count for much that capitalist performance on many fronts is manifestly superior to that of communism. What matters is that communism has demonstrated the mutuality and historic transiency of our particular social order, and that social order can never again feel entirely secure in its claims to permanence and legitimacy."

That is a profound thought and a dangerous one. In sports, one of the factors of the game is psychology. If you can make your opponent doubt himself, you have achieved the advantage. The same can hold true in political and economic thought. Unlike communism, which was masterminded by two men, capitalism has evolved through many great minds. The first to write on the subject of capitalism was Adam Smith. His classic book is entitled, *The Wealth of Nations*, and the quote he is famous for states, "Led by an invisible hand to promote an end which was not part of his intention by pursuing his own interest, he frequently promotes that of the society more effectually than when he really intends to promote it. I have never known much good done by those who affected to trade for the public good."

To assist in a better understanding of capitalism, its components should be reviewed. Economics tend to discuss economic theory using models. In capitalism, the model would include the concept of the competitive market sequence. Let's view our economy as a series of markets, in each of which a product or service is traded. It is important to remember, there are so many people who participate in the exchange of these products and services that no one person or organization can dominate the entire market.

The market is a mystery even to the most brilliant. Sure, there are indicators that can help predict movement, but the market concept itself is indeed fascinating. The book *Hidden Face of Free Enterprise* informs us, "The market system tells him he should, dares him to try. From the beginning, businesses have tried to escape from the whim of the market place. They have sought to control the market, and not have it control them. But, how do you control the market? You can't make people buy what they don't want. You can't fix a price for your product when someone else can sell the same item for less; when a foreign producer can invade your market. In a market system price is the key to success. Price is represented by the cost to produce, promote a product, and earn a predetermined net profit. It can be compared to a thermostat which assists in the gathering of all the information to conclude the results of a product's success, which is where you will find the essence of a free enterprise system.

Capitalism belongs to the private sector. A government program will never out-perform the private enterprise. Take time to study and learn about the economic system you operate under in our country. The more knowledge you gain, the more you will appreciate it and protect it.

Super Objective

"The right name which crystallizes the essence of a unit discovers its fundamental objective."

- Constantin Stanislavski

Stanislavski, in his many works and teachings, stressed that without the benefit of worthwhile playwrights, the theater would be nonexistent. The same applies to the sales presentation. If the script which we use as sales people is not current or meaningful, then all the talent in the world will not get the job done.

The sales presentation should be well thought out and reflect the company's goals and objectives. This can be accomplished using Stanislavski's principle of the super objective. The super objective, according to Sonia Moore in her book, *The Stanislavski System*, points out that, "the essence of the play must guide the director and the interpretation of characters and events. With the super objective, an actor weaves the author's ideas into the theatrical performance."

She continues, "The super objective is the basic stimulus of the creative process; the theatrical form and the written play should unite through a continual fertilization of each other in the process of building a performance. The super objective controls each character's logic of actions, which makes the theme concrete."

Many sales people feel that they have no real control in this area of sales content. However, if selling is your chosen profession and you are committed to your company, then it is critical that you analyze the content of the presentation. When carefully studied, does the presentation have a super objective? What is the purpose of the presentation? Does it address the needs of your clients?

According to Stanislavski, the objective of the theater was to portray the author's intent, and by doing so, one could bring to life the written text for the audience to digest through the actions of the actors and the director. The true meaning of the author's script must be communicated. The same thought should be instilled in the sales presentation.

If the saying that you get paid only for what you do is true, isn't it logical that if you do more than you are paid for, you will be paid more? Caring enough for your company to share insights with them is doing more than you are paid to do. Most companies would welcome suggestions from their field force dealing with sales content. The content should be based entirely on what the public wants and needs, and how your product will help them solve their dilemma. Most importantly, it will improve you in your role as a sales person.

Stanislavski said, "It's a good thing to have an objective, you cannot come out onto the stage to do something in general. On the stage, we must have life but not only that, it must be the life of your imagination which you make real for us. An actor himself must create that life, produce it through his fantasy. To be an actor, you must in the first instance, possess a developed, rich sense of fantasy. Your creativeness will begin only when you have in mind the words, if it were so without the magic if. Without fantasy, there can be no creativeness." This applies to selling, as well, in the sense that you need to reflect to the prospect your sense of well being which first begins in your own mind. You can't give away that which you don't first possess yourself.

Actors are people who play parts in the theater. Their parts are considered roles. Sales people are individuals who play parts for their companies. Why do I mention roles? You, as a sales professional, are consumed in a role for eight hours a day. You also play other roles in your life. For example, you may be a mother or father, you may be a friend and son or daughter. We all play different roles in life. The point of this illustration is to focus on the fact that the actor in a scene who is insulted or rejected doesn't take that feeling home with him. Rather, he knows that he personally wasn't insulted; it was the role he played that took the abuse. Selling should be viewed in the same way. The rejections that you receive in the course of the day are not rejections of you, but only of the role you play. When you adopt this attitude, you will find that your energy level will remain high and you will remain fresh for your next performance.

You must be able to project the main idea of the sales presentation to your prospect. This is done by determining the actions necessary in building your role to reflect the super objective.

Stanislavski thought that an actor must contribute a name to his super objective, and that name should be an action verb. The feedback from the audience relies on that simple but powerful fact. Your sales presentation must have a central point, a central focus, a theme that will serve as a foundation for your presentation.

The concept of a thorough line of action ties your sales performance to a logical order, so that you can draw a line which will run through your role. By doing so, there is an active execution of the super objective.

For each meeting, you must have an objective. The sales presentation must lead to an end, and that end should be one of solving or preventing problems in your prospect's life.

The Super Magnetic Goal Setting Plan

"If you are not making the progress you want or are capable of making, it is because your goals are not clearly defined."

- Paul J. Meyer

Goal setting provides the path to attain an individual's utmost desire of his heart. Goal setting, by its very nature, creates a magnetic force which draws all things in the plans to it. It can also be likened to a wheel that can roll over all obstacles in its way.

Those are strong words, yet they are true, provided the goals are intensified by what I like to call the "Super Magnetic Goal Setting Plan." There have been many books and pep talks given on the subject of goal setting. The words seem to lack the conviction of what the true power of goal setting can do in the lives of millions.

I feel obligated to recognize Paul J. Meyer's efforts at educating individuals. Meyer wrote about the dynamics of goal setting in which he outlined the steps to goal setting. They are simple and easy to understand, and will serve as a foundation for which I will share the magic of the "Super Magnetic Goal Setting Plan."

The first part of the plan is the crystallizing of your thoughts. This is done by self evaluation. The example that best illustrates this point is to think of yourself as an automobile. You are the vehicle. Now you must determine where the auto is heading. Everyone should have an idea where they are going; yet statistics have shown that only about five percent plan their lives. The quote that Paul J. Meyer is most known for, states, "If you are not now making the progress you'd like to make and are capable of making, it is simply because your goals are not clearly defined." My favorite quote is, "If you don't know where you are going, any road will take you there." If you don't know where you are going, how do you know when you have arrived? We all agree that knowing where you are going is important.

Also, everyone should live by a set of priorities, for without priorities there is no focus. Where there is no focus, there is no concentration. Without concentration, there can be no intensified efforts. In the absence of intensified efforts, there exists mediocrity.

The next part of the goal is to develop a course of strategy and time limits for completion. When the subject of planning is brought up, I can't help but think of my grandfather and those long hot summers when I worked as a "gopher" on the job site.

Before we set foot on the land, my grandfather had already built the house in his mind. He captured the idea of the house on blueprints. The blueprints ensured that the house was as good as done.

The second part of the plan was setting a deadline. There are really two reasons for setting a time frame on the goal. The first reason is to get started, and the second is to finish.

The third step is the development of a sincere desire. Desire is an amazing part of the human engineering makeup. No one can tell how much desire you have. No one knows how much desire you possess right now. Actions can reflect some degree of desire, but not conclusively. All great things accomplished started with desire. All the talent and ability will shrink and fade away without the magic motion of desire.

"The magic word desire was on the firmest bridges to the truth of real life; for human existence is an infinite chain of wishes and anxieties, and at any moment of his conscientious life is either striving towards something or trying to get away from it," Stanislavski is quoted as saying to his actors. He wanted to tap in to the actors' rich experiences instead of relying on pure emotion. The process to be followed to produce real emotions was found in the seeds of desire."

Attaining an abundance of belief in yourself and your abilities is the fourth step. If you don't believe in yourself, how can you expect anyone else to do so? When you believe you can do something, it actually becomes easier to do a particular task. The powerful affirmation pertaining to this mode of thinking states that, "When you know, and you know that you know, confidence replaces fear." Belief in yourself should be designed by self awareness which will expand with life experiences. Challenge is fueled by determination. I bought a plaque for my father many years ago for Father's Day. It read:

"Challenge"

"Every man has the ability within to do great things. His touchstone is challenge. No matter what his field of endeavor, he must measure himself against the demands of his world, to rise to the challenge. Ultimately, this is why men build bridges, climb mountains, and do a thousand other things that manifest personal achievement and satisfaction."

Determination gives you the power to want to win. With winning comes freedom. When freedom blooms, independence is achieved, yet freedom in all of its glory falls short of man's inner freedom within himself. Independence grows from peace of mind and tough mental thinking.

You have constructed your foundation with the guidelines outlined; now comes the time to build the structure that will serve to comfort you and your loved ones all the days of your lives.

You have analyzed and evaluated yourselves and have your thoughts organized so that you know where you want to go. You capture those thoughts of your aspiration by writing them down and assigning a time frame in which to reach them. You have taken your temperature, measured your own personal desire level, and have determined that, yes, you do want to accomplish the goal. You are committed to paying the price to get it. You believe that you have the ability to pull it off and the confidence level to sustain you in those insecure moments of goal attainment. You are a soldier dedicated to never giving up, never retreating from battle.

Now you are ready to proceed to the next part of fully understanding the power of goal setting. It is called action planning within the framework of your goal. Tom Fatjo, in his book entitled, *With No Fear Of Failure*, wrote, "Action planning really is: taking a goal, any size goal, and breaking it down into separate tasks or requirements which will lead to its accomplishment. Each task or requirement then becomes a smaller goal and devising action plans for each. We have a complete road map which shows the way from the starting point to the final achievement."

When you link action planning with your goals programs, you add the "super" into the goal setting plan. When you develop action plans with your goal setting plan, you ensure the success of your aspirations.

The benefits of direction and focus are accomplished by first charting the particular actions necessary in the accomplishment of your stated goal.

You pinpoint every element of the plan. First, release the power of your imagination. Action planning begins when you write, on the top of your page, the goal you want to accomplish, then list all the necessary steps to carry out the goal. I will illustrate an example. Your goal may be to write $250,000 on a new business this year.

Goal:

- Write $250,000 of new business in my store.

Steps:

- Arrange a meeting with the manager to discuss the plan.

- Develop a business plan to encompass all plans.

- Develop marketing plans, including the merchandise specials, promotions, and advertising.

- Sales training of the in-house people to ensure sales results.

- Financing of the new inventory.

- Expansion of the store space to accommodate additional products.

- Time commitment to fulfill goal; June 15, 1997.

The ideas will hit you in all the different areas of your particular business. Write down everything you can think of. Remember, it does not have to be in any particular order at this stage. Concentrate only on ideas generation.

After you've completed this step, go back and, here is that word again, prioritize your ideas in a logical order. For our example, let's assume you have your list in the correct order. The next step is, break down the goal into smaller goals.

Example: Financing New Inventory -

- Get all financial records including tax returns, financial statements, etc.
- Prepare a business plan for the bank.
- Write the proposal on the type of financing required, including rates, terms, etc.
- Set up a meeting with the loan officer.
- Time goal - all these things will be accomplished by January 15, 1997.

The exciting part of this type of program is, you are "brain-storming." Brainstorming means thinking of new creative ideas at the same time as you are planning the activity necessary to accomplish the goal.

All of these elements of goal setting are interrelated. The interpersonal part of yourself is reviewed. Goals are formulated with action plans, which leads to the final stage of "Super Magnetic Goal Setting."

A mathematician named Thomas Hobbes, who lived in the 1700's, was a fascinating gentleman. His analysis of the power of government and man's rights were years ahead of his time. Although many of his ideas were controversial and still are today, some of his thoughts are so profound and provoking, that it would be an injustice not to include some of them as they pertain to the "Super Magnetic Goal Setting Plan." Mr. Hobbes felt that the movement of physical bodies is the origin of all knowledge and thought. Furthermore, sensation, emotion, and reason are derivatives and results of motion.

However, the most interesting thought of Mr. Hobbes was, "The shift from reliance upon impulse to dependence upon reason does not alter the goal of behavior, which remains individual benefit and self preservation; it merely substitutes a superior for an inferior method of achieving that goal."

Mr. Hobbes' thoughts on the importance of motion are an intriguing part of the "Super Magnetic Goal Setting Plan." Thoughts are stimulated many times by motions. The mere physical action can influence your train of thought. The concept of motion is incorporated in the goals program.

After the origination and organizing of thoughts followed by the planning of actions, it is time to magnetize that goal and transform it into achievement. This is done by visualization. Visualization means that you not only see in your mind's eye that which you want to accomplish, but you also experience the feelings that come from attainment of the goal.

First, review your goal. This procedure must be followed very carefully. It involves a physical action. Sit or lie down at a time and in a place without interruptions. Begin the process of magnetizing by getting your body completely relaxed. Count to five. While counting, tighten your fists and legs, then your entire body. At the count of five, hold that tight position for an additional count of five. While tightening up, take the five count to get completely flexed. Slowly release that tension to the count of five. You will experience relief that will assist you in reaching relaxation. Now breathe deeply and hold it to the count of five. Release it to the count of ten. As you do this two more times, you should be feeling better than you have in months. Keep your hands at your sides and place your index finger on your thumb and breathe deeply from your diaphragm. In your mind's eye, see the word T-H-I-N-K. Focus your attention on that word. Remember the goal recorded. Watch yourself doing the very thing you have been planning to do. Experience the feeling that you receive in your visualization. See yourself as a winner. You thought of your goal, you planned your goal, and now you are rehearsing your goal mentally.

Studies have proven that athletes who practice mentally perform better than their counterparts who do not.

We are not through. The touching of your index finger to your thumb will trigger that feeling you were experiencing in your visualization. That is so powerful, so mysterious, yet is so true. You must reinforce the emotions in your visualization to attain the needed results. Incorporate this idea on the sub- goals in your action planning to obtain your main objective, or as Stanislavski called it, "The Super Objective."

Goal setting is a power that is available to you to assist in reaching your predetermined goals. It transforms ideas from mere thought impulse into their physical equivalent. The fact that you thought of something proves that you can have it; otherwise, your mind would have rejected the notion.

There is an abundance of success in the world awaiting you, but before you can have your share, you must discover the abundance of potential in yourself. This is accomplished by incorporating the "Super Magnetic Goal Setting Plan" into your life.

The Method of Physical Action

"Physical action is the bait for emotion,
a pretext for involving the psychological life."

- Constantin Stanislavski

The foundation of Stanislavski's system is based on the method of physical action. In Stanislavski's research and teachings he uncovered the existence of a strong bond that united the psychological and the physical in everyone. Thus, this theory states that there is a psychological reason behind all physical action. Its contention is that physical action will not be present without mental experiences. In reference to the written word, Stanislavski said, "That the word is the physical side of the psychophysical process; images and the meaning behind the words form its psychological side."

Communicate Your Sales Objective

Sales people have specific objectives that they set forth in their presentations. Communicating objectives through actions is a sales person's primary goal initially. We become less effective as sales people when we try to force our own emotions on our prospects. Stanislavski teaches that the more we try to drive the emotion outward, the less likely we are to get the other person to respond to it. The key, according to Stanislavski, is to "act logically and truthfully," and this applies in a sales presentation. We must communicate the true meaning through dialog, as well as in our physical actions. We must be conscious of the fact that they are working together. Stanislavski thought that a person's inner world is revealed through his or her physical action.

The initial purpose of Method Selling is to help you become aware of the fact that too often we project only the outward, superficial part of ourselves. Secondly, it is to assist you in acquiring a rich understanding of the "total human selling process concept," that can be accomplished by using Stanislavski's teachings.

Stanislavski said, "I had made a great discovery and realized the old truism that the inner emotions of an actor on the stage before the thousands in the audience, and with the footlights turned on, were unnatural and the main obstacle to working in public...that in such a physical and spiritual state, one can only pose, perform, and seem to experience, but cannot possibly live or give himself up to feeling."

When sales people get into their sales "costumes," they sometimes leave their human qualities at the door; they leave their naturalism in their dressing room; they leave the essence of themselves out of the role all together.

Method Selling will give you an opportunity to use the principles of one of the world's best teachers in the theater, and to apply them to make you become a more believable, thus more successful, sales person. The Method Selling concepts will make you a much richer sales person, but not just in the monetary sense. Stanislavski also said, "Physical action is the bait for emotion, a pretext for involving the psychological life. All attention must be directed to the execution of physical actions, to their logical consecutiveness. Only truthful, concretely executed physical actions, indispensable in the given circumstances, involve true emotions. The small truth of physical actions stirs the great truth of thought, emotions, experiences, and a small untruth of physical actions gives birth to a great untruth in the region of emotions, thoughts, and imagination." The seed of the thought impulse gives root to the physical action which reflects the inner dialogue occurring within ourselves.

Positive Thinking Works

This is a good time to reinforce the belief in the positive thought process. Think of yourself as a factory for a moment. Someone asks you, "What are you producing?" You respond with the famous example, "Widgets." He then asks whether or not there is a market for widgets in this area. You think for a moment and say, "No, there is not. I never thought about that. What a waste of money." That is what happens when we produce a negative thought. It serves no useful purpose, but just weakens our performance.

Everything in nature is positive, so anything that is negative stops the process of growth.

You must alter negative thoughts by first generating the psychological side of yourselves in an energetic, positive way, which will then give rise to the circumstances leading to the desired outcome. You must be on guard against all excessive movement which is not a part of the main objective. All this does is distract your prospect and weaken your believability in his eyes. A genuine action cannot be feigned, or unnecessary, because it reflects a true emotional feeling; whereas, false movements have no inner justification for their use, thus they appear as excessive. Stanislavski stressed, "The true, purposeful psychophysical action comes when the movement is justified inwardly."

Physical Action

Stanislavski's latest works moved away from the theory of stirring emotions intuitively to arrive at the creative state and began to explore the impact of physical action. Physical action results in a reflex that will trigger the emotions that you need to express a convincing presentation. An excellent example of this theory would be the idea of anchoring, used by mental health professionals. Try this experiment to gain a full understanding of the concepts. Place your hand on the arm or shoulder of someone. Ask the person to think of something that made him or her them happy. Leave your hand on the person while he or she is thinking about the event. Take your hand off and talk about something different. After a few minutes place your hand in the same location as you had previously.

Do you realize that by touching your friend or partner again he or she will immediately flashback to the feelings experienced while you touched the person the first time. Stanislavski felt that physical action can and will influence your inner self, which will affect your outer life performance.

Method Selling teaches you to work with your prospects automatically as human beings. In understanding the power of realism, you no longer depend on chance. To quote from Stanislavski, "For chance, as every artist knows, is the enemy of art." Never leave your success to chance. Insure it by mastering the elements of physical action.

Stanislavski devised nine elements of action which will be covered in the lessons to follow. They are: Magical If, Given Circumstances, Imagination, Concentration of Attention, Truth and Belief, Communion, Adaptation, Tempo-Rhythm and Emotional Memory. Digest them one at a time to get the full benefit of each lesson. Use the power of repetition when you study the lessons so that the messages can become a part of your individual makeup.

Elements of Physical Action

"On the stage, we must have life but not only that, it must be the life of your imagination which you make real for us. An actor himself must create that life, produce it through his fantasy."

- Constantin Stanislavski

Imagination

"Imagination creates things that can be or can happen and every movement you make on the stage, every word you speak, is the result of the right life of your imagination," said Stanislavski.

Everyone has the wonderful gift of an imagination. It has been given to us free and clear, yet most people have not fully realized the power of their own imaginations.

Imagination for Creative Living

Imagination has been defined as a "conscious idea or mental image of something never before wholly perceived in reality." In order to create, you must first mentally create in your imagination. That is a remarkable fact. A quick look into your life will show that you would have never entered the world of selling, if that picture was not one of success. Imagination is one of the most important traits that a sales person possesses.

Napoleon Hill, in his classic book, *Think and Grow Rich* said, "Man's only limitation, within reason, lies in his development and use of his imagination." When you have polished imagination, you can think of new ways to attract and keep clients. The "Magic If," another element of Stanislavski's system, can exist only within a rich, fertile imagination.

Stanislavski wrote on the subject of the feeling of imagination, "In it there is the play of imagination and the creation of creative faith; in it there is a barrier against scenic lies; in it is the feeling of true measure; in it is the tree of childlike naivete and sincerity of artistic emotions." Sales people need to turn on the emotions in their presentations through the use of their imaginations, which will bring the presentation to life.

William James, the Father of Psychology, taught us that people are not only subject to action through logic, but also are always moved through emotions.

Emotions start with you in the form of a thought impulse that you originate in your own mind and which makes up your imagination. With your mind, you can observe the world. In sales training workshops, I discuss the look and listen strategy that teaches us to be fully aware of the body language of the prospect, and listen not only to what prospects say, listen to how they say it. Take it a step beyond and listen to what they are not saying. That is where your imagination comes into play in your presentation.

The Wonder of Your Mind

Harold Sherman felt that the mind has the ability to receive, to disperse and to activate changes that came in the impulse of an idea or impression - which the mind translates through the experience into the growth and success of an individual. He went on to write that the mind is indeed the only property in the entire universe which maintains its identity and which grows by changes within and without itself.

Your mind is truly an important part of your mental makeup. Although, its been given to you free as standard equipment, it's development can improve your life immensely. Practice using your imagination. A good practice exercise would be to visualize beautiful scenes you have viewed in your travels. Next, visualize places you have never seen, creating the scenic sights in your mind. Try to hold these thoughts for five minutes. You will find as for all human activities, the more you use your imagination, the easier it becomes.

Magic If

"From the time when the "If" appears, the actor is carried away from the plan of real life to that of the life he is imagining."

- Constantin Stanislavski

The second element of physical action is the Magic If. Many times in our daily lives we have to work with unfamiliar people. In meeting new people there is always present in one or both parties a defense barrier. This next element is an excellent way to help you overcome this common obstacle in the introduction phase of selling.

In his book, *My Life In Art*, Stanislavski writes, "I came to understand that creativeness begins from that moment when in the soul and imagination of the actor there appears the magical, creative 'if'. From the moment of the appearance of 'if', the actor passes from the plane of another life, created and imagined by himself. Believing in this life the actor can begin to create."

Use the Playground in Your Mind

The concept is simple when fully understood. The Magic If, as Stanislavski coined it, will add new life into your intent. The content of the sales presentation will become your content. Magic If is a reinforcer to the deeper subconscious and to your outside actions. This element will provide you with better results in your endeavors. When you are working with your prospect, ask yourself the question, "What if this person were a family member? Would I sound different? Would my body respond in a more relaxed style?" We know in our reality that this person is not a family member, but by acting "as if" the person were, we can project the truth of our convictions in our product in a more convincing powerful way. When we use the wonder of our thoughts with the triggering of power through the Magic If, then we can set in motion the operation of our ideas, which will lead to the actions necessary to wake up our emotions. Those emotions are critical to making your prospects become clients. According to Stanislavski, "To achieve this kinship between the actor and the person he is portraying add some concrete detail which will fill out the play, giving it point and absorbing action. The circumstances which are predicated on *if* are taken from sources near to your own feelings, and they have a powerful influence on the inner life of an actor.

Once you have established this contact between your life and your part, you will feel that inner push or stimulus. Add a whole series of contingencies based on your own experience of life, and you will see how easy it will be for you sincerely to believe in the possibility of what you are called upon to do on the stage." This same principle applies in your role as a sales professional. Reminisce on your past experiences of helping people and connecting with others.

In Nikolai A. Gorchakov's book entitled, *The Theater in Soviet Russia*, he states that, "Timidly but persistently, Stanislavski kept seeking new links for his system. He discovered the magic formula of 'if'. Stanislavski considered when the if appears, the actor is carried away from the plane of real life to that of the life that he is imagining. Once he believes it, the actor can begin to work. The stage is the truth in which the actor sincerely believes, and even an obvious falsehood must become the truth in the theater in order to be art."

We must reflect this same attitude in our view of selling. Explore the Magic If in your presentation and in your life and discover the magic of the Magic If. Create the life that you want and are entitled to. It is your birthright.

Act As If

Using Stanislavski's concept of the Magic If will prove to be an effective way to build trust and rapport with your prospect. The "Act As If" concept will help you internalize the characteristics you want to possess, much like what the Magic If accomplishes with your prospect. The concept in a nutshell is to act as if you are already the person you want to become in the future.

If your goal is to be more assertive in your life, then simply act as though you are more assertive. Guess what magically happens? You become the very person you have chosen to create for yourself. If you want to be vice president of your company, start acting as though you are your company's vice president. People will notice the change in you and move you toward that position. In order to be something, you must first think and act.

When you become successful in sales, you open so many doors for the future. However, being a sales professional is a respected position and is just as important as a manager, vice president, or president of your company. Act as if you are the top salesperson in your organization, and watch the positive changes in your life.

Take a few minutes and list some of the traits you would like to possess. Now think about someone whom you know that has this particular trait. Watch and study their behavior. You will find this exercise to be most helpful in formulating your new behavior.

Role modeling is the most neglected form of learning in our society today. According to Richard Doss in his book, *Theory P,* "The absence of role models makes pursuit of improvement more difficult, and striving to maintain quality more tenuous. Having someone to look up to, be like, and follow helps improvement. Real-life examples of high achievers make the pursuit more enjoyable and improvement more easily attainable."

This by no means intended to make you feel inferior; rather it is a very effective way to assist you in developing into the person you want to be in the future. One mental game you can use to keep everyone on a level playing field is to think of an outstanding trait you have that your current role model does not possess. Also, you must remember that you too are a role model for others. Strive to be the best, and to do the right things right. You need to be a builder of people, and set a good example for others to follow in the course of your business and personal life. One of my favorite affirmations taken from my marital art master states that, "I am perfect because I never make mistakes knowingly." Use the concept of "acting as if" to project the right impression to your prospect.

Emotional Memory

"All such feelings are the results of something that has gone before. Of the thing that goes before you should think as hard as you can."

- Constantin Stanislavski

The profound truth is that the things that you remember were reinforced by emotion. That is why Stanislavski included the emotional memory as part of his elements of an action. Vernon Wolfe, in his program, "Unfolding Potential" wrote, "In order to improve memory, one method is to learn to experience things with more specific focus, more intensity."

Stanislavski wrote "All I'm telling you now is that because of the realm of the emotion, not of reason, you are feeling what I am saying more easily than understanding it."

Memory is a key trait in successful sales professionals for many reasons. First of all, you must memorize your presentation, responses to objectives, and conclusion statements. Secondly, it is important to remember your prospects, clients and your competitors.

Memory gives us an abundance of information to draw upon when we need it most. Memory is comprised of the education and experience that you have accumulated over your lifetime.

Stanislavski was said to be well versed in all areas of thoughts. Stanislavski knew how critical emotions were in his actors when he wrote, "Time is an excellent filter, an excellent purifier of memories or emotions once experienced. Moreover, time is an excellent artist. It not only purifies but is capable of poeticizing the memories."

Emotions are an intrinsic part of the selling process. As we discussed earlier, emotions initiate actions. In the discussion of emotions, Dr. George W. Crane wrote a book entitled *Applied Psychology*. In the book he wrote, "Remember, motions are the precursors of emotions. You can't control the latter directly but only through your choice of motions or actions...to avoid this all to a common tragedy (marital difficulties and misunderstandings) become aware of the true psychological fact. Go through the proper motions each day and you'll soon begin to feel the corresponding emotions! Just be sure you and your mate go through those motions of dates and kisses, the phrasing of sincere daily compliments, plus the many other little courtesies, and you need not worry about the emotion of love. You can't act devoted for very long without feeling devoted."

The Power of the Love Emotion

Love is the most powerful of all emotion, so with that bit of information we should make it a point to fill our day and mind with love thoughts.

Thoughts originate emotions, which lead to expressions through actions. Mr. Joseph Weed wrote an interesting passage on thoughts when he wrote, "For each thought out of the mundane will carry with it, and seemingly dripping from it, some of the emotional substance of its creator." That is a fascinating way of viewing the power of thoughts and emotions. In selling, we must not be afraid of using the power of emotions in communicating with our prospects. Og Mandino wrote *The Greatest Salesman in the World,* a best-seller. In the scroll marked "Two" he stressed the importance of love to the salesman when he wrote, "For this is the greatest secret of success in all ventures. Muscle can split a shield and even destroy life, but only the unseen power of love can open the hearts of men, and until I master this art, I will remain no more than a peddler in the market place. I will make love my greatest weapon and none on whom I call can defend against its force."

Stanislavski taught that when his actors were on stage they were experiencing only the memory of the emotion they were trying to communicate to the audience. In many of the plays, the actors were required to experience traumatic circumstances which would drive anyone to mental illness if it were reality. Sonia Moore wrote, "The actor is capable of stirring a needed emotion within himself only because he had often experienced an analogous emotion in his own life. Every experience in life leaves traces on our central nervous system, and thus the nerves which participate in a given experience become more sensitive to such a stimulus."

Vernon Wolfe in his work, *Unfolding Potential*, writes about the reinforcers of memory. He outlines six areas which will help you in the understanding and development of your Emotional Memory. The six areas are:

1. **Focus:** The ability to recall depends upon whether you were able to focus specifically on a given event or fact. If you don't focus on the event, you have trouble recalling it.

2. **Intensity:** The greater the intensity of an event, the easier it is to recall. Think, for example, of some early trauma in your life. In most cases you will be able to recall the entire event in detail. You cannot only see, in your mind, what happened, but you can hear the sounds, feel the feelings, smell, taste and feel everything about it.

3. **Meaning:** Events which have the most meaning are the easiest to recall. Your mind keeps them closer to your conscious level of awareness. Your wedding is easier to remember, for example, than what you ate for breakfast the day before the wedding.

4. **Frequency:** Repetition increases your ability to recall. The more you repeat an event, the clearer your mind is able to assimilate all the facts for your instant recall.

5. **Newness:** The more recent the event, the more likely you are to recall it. Short term memory is transferred into long term holodigms as the body responds to input from the senses. Holodigms are complete from the first instant they are recorded. They become integrated into the living arena of the memory banks of your mind as time goes on.

6. **Verification:** Finding out you were right about something allows your mind to correlate its picture of reality. Things which do not correlate are often buried, outside of our conscious conform beliefs.

A simple acronym will help you to develop your Emotional Memory. Think of IRA which stands for: Impression, Repetition, Association. First, you must focus on the impression. Next, you repeat the object in your mind, followed by associating it with something you have already stored in your memory banks.

Your memory is your personal resource that will assist you in every situation you happen to find yourself. You can tap in on others' experiences that you have read and studied as well as your own experiences in similar events. Build depth in your emotional bank, so you can benefit from this valuable commodity.

Concentration of Attention

"The actor's work includes first of all, complete concentration of his entire spiritual and physical nature. It embraces not only sight and hearing but all five human senses."

- Constantin Stanislavski

We have found in studying human psychology that interest of any kind produces a natural concentration. Concentration is the ability to focus on one goal or objective in the midst of all the other things that are going on. When you have strong concentration, you heighten the level of your performance. Concentration will keep you on the correct path not only in your presentation, but also in your personal life.

As children, you may have used a magnifying glass to burn leaves. The sun, by itself, does not burn the leaves. However, when the sun's rays are intensified, they are capable of increasing in power. The same applies with human action. When you focus on your mental energies in a concentrated manner, then you are better able to accomplish that which you are seeking. Stanislavski pointed out the importance of concentration by including it in his elements of action. He pointed out in his teaching that his actors could perform without fear and could do it in a relaxed way. They could achieve this without the normal distractions by reaching what Stanislavski referred to as public solitude, as Sonia Moore describes in her work on Stanislavski. "This is possible if an actor gives maximum attention to the physical action and to all that his imagination is able to build around it. A concrete thought and a concrete physical action will hold the actor's attention. Fully concentrated attention depends on the thorough execution of the physical action."

Experiment with your sales script using concentrated attention for maximum expression. Focus on your physical action in your presentation and your thoughts as you perform it.

Lee Strasberg, an American gem in his own right, had this to say about concentration: "On the stage, if we are willing to concentrate on and give ourselves to a problem, we are already dealing with that problem. The willingness to go step by step without worry about whether you have the hundred percent is the big secret in acting. In the human being there is the expression when he is least concerned about it. The actor is an instrument that pays attention. Something happens to him as a result of paying attention, which is pure expression.

I'm not talking about energy. I'm not talking about volume. I'm not talking about strength of expression. I'm talking about the expressiveness which is part of the fundamental equipment of the human being - and therefore, of the actor." You possess the natural gift of expression. Ask yourself, do you try to impress your prospects, or do you express yourself to them? This mind shift will greatly improve your presentation.

John Malloy, best known as the author of *Dress for Success*, is also a productivity consultant. In his book, *How to Beat the Competition in the Ground*, he writes: "If you're starting to measure your ability to concentrate, you must understand that this ability will vary dramatically depending on a number of factors: whether you like or dislike the project, your state of mind, if you're worried or upset about something, how well you feel that day, or even if you're having an off day. In addition, familiarity with the subject will make concentration easier. Our research indicates that it is far more difficult to concentrate on a subject when it's first introduced. We also discovered that concentration connected with physical activity is dramatically different from concentration connected with purely mental activity."

He continues, "Before working on your concentration, you should measure your ability to focus, since some of the techniques used to improve concentration also help improve focus." As a sales professional, your ability to concentrate is an integral factor in making you effective in your presentation.

Develop Your Circle of Attention

Learning to concentrate will empower you as a sales professional. Your prospects will sense your intense interest in them. You will appeal to their most important needs, to be listened to and understood. Practice exercising your focus will improve your ability to concentrate. Learn to control the thoughts which enter your mind.

When you apply the elements of Method Selling, you will evolve to heighten awareness. In this stage you are in complete control of everything in your life, and you will surround yourself and others with universal tranquility.

Stanislavski had a unique view on concentration that is very effective. He called it the circles of attention and taught that to facilitate concentration it was necessary to incorporate physical actions. The first circle was referred to as the small circle of attention which consisted of one or two persons and objects. The goal of the actor was to be the center of the area and, by doing so, could have his attention drawn to the contents inside the area.

The next area was called the medium circle of attention, which was an area that could encompass a couple of people and larger objects such as furnishings. The goal here was to expand his concentration into the larger area. The emphasis was not to engulf the entire area; rather, this should be done at a graduated pace.

The last and final circle of attention is everything in sight of the actor. As in life, the larger the area, the harder it is to focus. Yet, sometimes it is required of us to take in the big picture. Stanislavski taught that when you feel you are drifting from the subject, you should concentrate on a small immediate object and focus in on it until you have regained your attention. The sales person who can master concentration will be activated and alert and will be in a stronger position to work with the prospect. Remember that concentration is a natural part of your life. You are involved in it every day and in varying degrees. In order to be fully focused, ask yourself the "what and the why" behind all of your actions.

After your imagination has mentally created the mood and feelings that are required for you to reflect and to persuade the client, you must focus on the presentation. This is done by concentration. Stanislavski said that, "Concentration, creativeness is first of all the complete concentration of the entire nature of the actor."

Napoleon Hill wrote in his book *Think and Grow Rich*, "A jack of all trades seldom is good at any. Concentrate all of your efforts on one definite chief aim."

Concentrate on one objective in your presentation. Covering too many areas will water down the result. Practice concentrating; it is a trait that can be developed. A simple exercise would be to focus on a flame of a candle for a few minutes. Concentrate only on the flickering of the flame. The benefit to you is an increase in the ability to hold your thoughts on a particular endeavor.

Learn to Concentrate

It is possible to learn concentration? Ernest Dimnet wrote, "Concentration, which at first sight is obtained by elimination, the elimination of images not harmonious with our train of thought, can best be obtained by the conjuring of a suitable background. This background is nothing else than the manipulation of harmonious images."

Dimnet went on the say, "On the whole, concentration is a natural state which can easily be reproduced by simple methods. It is supposed to be exceptional because people do not try, and, in this, as in so many other things, starve within an inch of plenty. Those who do not try have never been disappointed in the process, but by some things experienced disappointment in themselves."

In closing, Stanislavski pointed out that, "Intensive observation of an object naturally arouses a desire to do something with it. To do something with it in turn intensifies your observation of it. This mutual inter-reaction establishes a stronger contact with the object of your attention ... in watching acting of great artists ... their creative inspiration is always bound up with their concentration of attention..."

The knowledge you gain by learning to concentrate will enable you to accomplish your goals, and will make you a more powerful persuader by increasing your ability to listen accurately to your prospect. Practice focusing on the circle of attention in your world. You will find that there is so much you have been missing.

Given Circumstances

*"Drama implies that there is something
we have to know in order to
understand what is happening now."*

- Lee Strasberg

Another element of physical action is the given circumstances. "The given circumstances," according to Sonia Moore, "is the plot of the play, the epoch, the time and place of the action, the conditions of life, the director's and the actor's interpretation, the setting, the properties, lighting, sound effects - all that an actor encounters while he creates a role."

In the given circumstances, Stanislavski said that the Magic If is the starting point, the given circumstances, the development. In given circumstances, you take into account all the circumstances that you interact with in the selling situation.

Many sales people's psychological and physical behaviors are subject to the external influences of their environment. An action makes clear what certain characters do in a given situation. You need to be familiar with your surroundings so that you actually become a part of them.

Truth and Belief

"This is the actor's task, then - to create people and incidents or happenings that seem so real at the time that the audience can enter into the spirit of the play and truly believe in what they see while it is happening."

- Elizabeth Y. Kelly

Stanislavski, in his writings, points out to his actors that, "The reality of the inner life of a human spirit is a part of and a belief in that reality. We are not concerned with the actual naturalistic existence of what surrounds us on the stage, the reality of the material world. This is of use to us only in so far as it supplies a general background for our feelings." When you are performing a presentation, search for your sense of truth. When you find truth, you will uncover your sense of faith that will allow you to justify your actions in the development of your role as a professional sales person. Stanislavski emphasized that you find truth bit by bit, finding your action on the simplest, physical basis.

The truth is a very powerful part of every presentation when it is magnetic through physical action. Truth and belief are two very important components in the selling process. In selling, you must believe in truth and reflect it in everything that you say and do. A comic once claimed he didn't lie because he would have to remember too much. When you understand the surge of strength that comes from the belief that something is true, you will find that your persuasion becomes irresistible. As an actor, one must portray events and individuals as people want to believe they are. In the world of selling, the beliefs that we share must be what the prospect believes them to be.

According to Nikolai Gorchakov's book, *The Theater in Soviet Russia;* reads: "Seek the truth of simple physical actions that are obvious to you. The truth of physical actions leads you to faith; everything goes further into the 'I am'. It flows into action and creative work. The method of physical actions enables an actor to acquire faith, to penetrate into the realm of authentic emotions and profound experiences. He creates a stage character in the shortest way possible."

You can also create a character that is both convincing and sincere to persuade the prospect of the benefits of your product.

Make each presentation as though it is the first time that you have performed it. By doing so, you will breathe new energy into it, which will create the results that you are seeking.

In conclusion Stanislavski said, "Our only concern is that all we do should be in the direction of developing and strengthening this sense. It is a difficult task because it's so much easier to lie when you are on the stage than to speak and act the truth. You will need a great deal of attention and concentration to aid the proper growth of your sense of truth and to fortify it." When you become a product of the product, that is, to be a user of the product or service, you can generate a great deal of conviction to your prospect. Use the power of truth in everything you do because the truth will stimulate you and your productivity to greater heights.

Communion

"He wanted the system to provide the means whereby
an actor could embody the spirit or 'incarnation'
of a role and give it the most human form obtainable."

- Ned Manderino

Communion, or communication, as we call it in this country, is the basis of all interpersonal relationships. Communication is not limited to just the verbal part of our speech; rather, it encompasses all forms of communication. This includes the body, the face and mannerisms.

According to Larry Barker, "The communication process is a system that involves an interrelated, interdependent group of elements working together as a whole to achieve a desired outcome or goal." Stanislavski made it part of his "Elements of Action." The spoken word reveals and reflects all of the inner and outer dialogue of the individuals in a situation. He knew the power of the spoken word when he wrote, "Words should become a means, not an end." He went on to say, "Words are not an end in themselves. We shall first learn to move about, to act. Any routine actor can recite his role, that's not difficult to learn. He can have as many cliche intonations as he will have automatic muscular reaction. But what we have to learn is how to move, how to sing, or dance, or mime, whether we use actual words or not."

Focus on Total Communication

In communication, most of the actual content takes place outside the verbal content. For example, it has been noted that the majority of communication is expressed through the face, body and mannerisms of the players. In the world of selling, the same principles apply. Anyone can memorize a sales presentation. The key is whether you can recite it as your words and with your style. I've heard it said that personal style is being yourself, but being yourself on purpose. As Mae West said, "It's not what you say, it's how you say it. It is not what you do, it's how you do it."

Communicate with Your Prospect

Stanislavski pointed out in his teaching that when his actors had contact with the audience, they would, many times, become more like reporters than actors. In selling, sales people sometimes read their presentation as though it were a monologue. There is no communication going on between the sales person and the prospect. It has the "all me" attitude. The presentation should be a communication process that is focused on the client's needs and wants. Sonia Moore pointed out an interesting fact concerning Stanislavski: "As our behavior in life depends on people around us, the actor's behavior as a character is related to that of the people around him; he has different relationships with those, for instance, who are friendly and with those who are hostile. His use of the 'Magic If' and/or his imagination will help him to develop the proper attitudes toward each of his fellow actors."

This brings back memories of a humorous story of a husband and wife who are sitting down, talking when the wife said, "Of course you don't understand me, Fred, because you listen to what I say instead of what I mean."

The key in selling is for the sales professional to create affinity with the prospect. Affinity is the alikeness of two objects. In our example, it is you and the prospect who are uniting. You create affinity by first relating similar interests, experiences, or sharing similar friendships with the prospect. Secondly, you should mirror the body position of the prospect, i.e., sitting, standing, legs crossed, hands on hips.

Lastly, is the verbal affinity, which is matching the "speech sense" of the prospect. All these things will help improve your role as a person who can relate to the prospect, who cares about the prospect, who understands the prospect; and who can help prospects solve or prevent problems in their lives.

Creating Affinity through Language

Communication provides a fascinating facet to the selling process. Did you know you can also create affinity in your choice of words with your prospects? It is important to create affinity early in the presentation. Were you aware that people communicate through their senses? In fact, all that we have learned came to us through our five senses. By listening to your prospect you can determine what sense is his or her dominant sense. With this information, you can then mirror their "speech sense" to create verbal affinity. Some solid examples of this will help clarify this thought.

The prospect who is dominated by the visual sense will indicate this by responding, "Oh, I see what you mean." When you hear those words, show the benefit to your prospect. You would say "... Let's look at the investment in..." These are excellent examples in creating verbal affinity with the visual prospect.

Those prospects who are audio dominated would say, "I heard that the machines only last for a year or so..." Hearing those words, you could respond, "Once you hear about the warranty..." The prospect who is taste oriented would say something like, "This proposal gives me a bad taste in my mouth." You would say, "The sweetest part of the proposal is the financing of the..."

The touch dominated prospect would respond, "I feel that the contract is too long." Hearing those words, you would reply, "I want to touch on the time frame with you..."

The smell dominated prospect said, "Something about this product smells fishy to me...," once again, you would say, "We are a company with fresh ideas when it comes to working with a company such as yours."

Persuasion Is an Action Word.

Persuasion is an element of communion. Persuasion is the tool used by actors and sales people to accomplish their particular objectives. It is of utmost importance to fully understand the fundamentals of persuasion. First of all, when discussing persuasion, we are not describing an adjective. It has been defined as, "a persuading or being persuaded; power of persuading; a strong belief; conviction."

Action is the buzz word in selling. Stanislavski felt that action on the stage must create something. He went on to say that, "Motion is the basis of the art ... of the actor ... even external immobility ... does not imply passiveness. You may sit without motion and at the same time be in full action ... frequently physical immobility is the direct result of inner intensity. So I will ... put it like this: on the stage it is necessary to act, either outwardly or inwardly. Everything that happens on the stage has a definite purpose. All action in the theater must have an inner justification, be logical, coherent and real ... and as a final result, we have a truly productive activity..."

In our selling life we should always have an objective. Persuasion is the energizing of our objective or goal. It provides the fuel to lead us to our destination. Persuasion consists of the specific words and actions that communicate to our prospects the necessary information to lead them to their final decision. Persuasion is the power of your personality, which tells the world who you are. To enhance your ability to become more persuasive remember the acronym, CHIEF, which stands for: Caring, Humor, Interest, Empathy, and Friendliness..

Caring

Persuasion is accomplished by the simple but honest action of caring. Caring is the psychological focus on another person's individual needs. Caring may sound a lot like empathy, but remember, empathy is seeing the world through the eyes of the other. However, caring is the sincere inner desire to help others either in the physical, mental, or emotional sense.

In a seminar presented by the American Heart Association, there was a young lady from a motivation company who opened the meeting with an acronym for the word "care." The "C" stood for customer. The "A" represented attention. The "R" stood for require, and "E" represented effort. Let's put it all together. The customer's attention requires effort. That effort starts with a caring attitude toward the other person.

Earl Nightingale, in his series "Insight", said, "It takes courage to care, to open your heart and react with sympathy, or compassion, or indignation, or enthusiasm when it is easier, and sometimes safer, not to get involved. But people who take the risk, who deliberately discard the armor of indifference, make a tremendous discovery: the more things you care about, and the more intensely you care, the more alive you become." He went on to say that another definition for enthusiasm is passionate caring.

The power of caring is best illustrated in the philosophy of helping others in hopes that by doing so you will get what you want. However, the initial purpose is to help the others solve or prevent problems that you or your product or service can accomplish.

People in general don't care how much a sales person knows about his or her product. What they do care about is how much the sales person cares about them.

Humor

Humor is not only an ice breaker, but it usually has a valve that releases tension that has built up in the beginning of the sales presentation. It must be realized that a joke and humor are very different. Jokes are not recommended for the simple fact that they are isolated dialogue that most likely doesn't fit into your super objective. Humor, on the other hand, allows you to share insight into an idea that you are trying to convey to your prospect, but it does so in a humorous way. When your prospect laughs or even smiles, his or her mind has opened up to you. A good sense of humor doesn't mean that you are a comedian or that you know every joke in town. What it does mean is that you are easy to be around, and you are light hearted. Moreover, it reveals that you have an unique view of life, choosing to interpret it through a positive humorous train of thought.

Interest

Interest is an element in persuasion. When you equip yourself with interest, you will stand a better chance of influencing your prospect. Interest has been defined as "unsatisfied curiosity." The reason we grow tired of people, places, and things is that we quit asking questions about them. Once we have satisfied our curiosity, we lose all interest in those things. Interest is the starting point where all persuasion begins. Interest is what unites the two individuals in the persuasion presentation. The interest should be to make the meeting a win/win situation. All the elements of persuasion grow out of interest.

Empathy

We have heard that old worn cliche that "empathy is walking a mile in the other man's moccasins." Empathy walks on long after the moccasins have worn out. Empathy is getting into the prospect's mind to experience the world from his or her point of view, not yours. Empathy should be incorporated into everything with which we come in contact. Whether it is reviewing a political issue or disciplining a child, it is wise to stop, even if only for a moment, and view yourself and your actions through others' eyes.

This exercise will do more to improve your performance not only in selling, but also in your personal relationships. Empathy, put another way as pertaining to selling, is to sell *the way you* want to be sold.

You must never forget to view your prospect as a magnificent functioning human being who is seeking and needing the service and the products which you are marketing.

Friendliness

When we think of a persuasive person, friendliness doesn't usually enter the picture; however, the truth is that an element of persuasion is the art of being friendly. People don't like to be forced into accepting an idea. When you are friendly, it melts away the defensiveness of your prospects. It makes the whole exchange of ideas much more pleasant. Friendliness is powerful; yet, unlike other types of powerful traits, this one can exist only by giving it away. If you desire to gain this trait, you must first share it. Remember, the best way to have a friend is to be a friend. It is actually easier to be friendly than to be a stuffy person.

Master the art of persuasion by reading and studying the research from others and incorporate these helpful ideas into your daily walk through life.

Learn the steps necessary to attain the power of persuasion in your life, and become the CHIEF of your world.

Tempo-Rhythm

"However, right tempo and true expression are related to the demands of dramatist's material as well as the technical reality of the right actor."

- Lee Strasberg

All of the elements of actions are interrelated. The element to be discussed here is called the Tempo-Rhythm. As indicated by the name, it implies the speed of an action. The pace of a certain activity dictates, many times, the outcome of the activity. The Tempo-Rhythm is tied to the element of given circumstances, which gives the person the temperament to follow though with the action.

The modern form of exercising is aerobics. In this form of exercise, you move to music. In the same vein, Stanislavski loved music very deeply and spent a great deal of time on the improvement of the opera. He stated, "From the instant the music begins, you are completely in its power. Your nerves, blood, heartbeat must all be in accord with the rhythm, live with it, let it permeate your whole being. It is the thing that carries away your emotions, arouses them, giving them both keenness and power."

In a sketch of his system, Stanislavski had originally listed 40 parts to his system. He had written down as number 24, the "Finishing of Problems (beats) and Master in Movement." Yet, he listed "Tempo-Rhythm" as number 29. As the years progressed, I assume these two elements were merged.

In the discussion of movement, Stanislavski also referred to inner movement. In selling, it is very important that you match the Tempo-Rhythm of your prospect, at least in the beginning stages, to develop a similarity to them. Your movement must be orchestrated and flow smoothly to reflect your competency in your area of expertise. Always control your movements, and don't fall into the trap of having unconscious body movements. This will distract from your super objective and will make your presentation less effective.

Get in Rhythm with Your Prospect

Tempo-Rhythm is reflected not only in your physical movement, but in your speech as well. Stanislavski said, "Many actors who are careless of speech, inattentive to words, pronounce them with such thoughtless slipshod speed, without putting any endings on them, that they end up with completely mutilated, half spoken phrases." Sales professionals are no exception to this fault.

In our busy day, we sometimes forget that the purpose of our day is seated right in front of us, and that our prospect deserves our full, concentrated attention. Stanislavski went on to say (about Tempo-Rhythm), "We think, dream, grieve about things to ourselves in a special Tempo-Rhythm because each moment is manifest in our lives. Wherever there is life, there is action; wherever action, movement; where movement, tempo; and where there is tempo, there is rhythm..." Find the rhythm in your sales presentation that will allow you to harness your power of persuasion.

It is known that Tempo-Rhythm does have the unusual property that can stimulate your mood. Tempo-Rhythm is not confined to the speed of an action; rather, it encompasses all the inner workings of the mind. Stanislavski also felt that immobility hindered performance. He said, "I had thought that immobility would allow me to devote all my energy and attention to the inner life of my role. As it turned out, this arbitrary immobility which was not based on any inner necessity gave rise to extreme tension and tautness of body and soul. This was quite understandable; faced with this arbitrary forcing of nature all feeling evaporated and was replaced by mechanical, cliche acting."

The key to being free from tension is accomplished through relaxation exercise which will be covered later. It is important for you to eliminate immobility from your behavior. You will find that being mobile can be so fulfilling when the word mobile is viewed as an acronym.

In this day and age, companies as well as sales people must be mobile, mobile in their thinking and in their physical apparatus. A trait of a top quality sales person is the ability to be mobile.

The term mobile is defined by the *American College Dictionary* as: Movable; moving readily, flowing freely, as a liquid; changing easily in expression, as features; quickly responding to impulses, emotions, etc. as the mind; versatile. The word mobile is a very enriching word and is an essential trait that everyone should possess.

For our discussion let us break up the word and study the term as a acronym. MOBILE - The "M" stands for motivation. The sales person must be motivated. Many sales people are interested in finding out where motivation comes from. Motivation in the purest sense of the word is psychological energy directed toward a goal. You find motivation when you create your goal, so write out your goal, focus on your purpose, couple it with action, and you will create motivation.

The "O" stands for optimism. It has been said that a pessimist has more of a realistic view of life. However, optimists live longer. Norman Vincent Peale wrote an interesting book entitled *The Tough-Minded Optimist*. In his book, Mr. Peale described optimism as: "The doctrine that the goods of life overbalance the pain and evil of it, that life is preponderantly good, the inclination to put the most favorable construction upon actions and happenings, minimize adverse aspects, conditions and possibilities, or anticipate the best possible outcome; a cheerful temperament." Does being optimistic really work? It has the attraction effect. Being optimistic often attracts optimistic circumstances, which lead to optimistic results.

The "B" represents busy. Everyone must stay busy in good times and in bad times. Activity is insurance against any chance of failing in the business of selling. Busy means working with your clients and servicing those clients, as well as securing new clients in the course of the day.

"I" represents intuition. Intuition has been said to be the elevated state of instinct. Instinct is the ability to know something without previous information, memory or experience. The animal kingdom has been blessed with this amazing instinct.

Human beings possess much higher degrees of instinct, called intuition. However, we have evolved by using our reasoning ability. Selling is not an instinctive element in life. Selling is a learned behavior which one can master upon study and practice. It is true that sales people can and will use their instinct in certain situations. With a reservoir of knowledge, one can radiate power with the confidence of knowing what to do and when to do it.

Relying on the higher intelligence will prove more reliable than on the primitive makeup of the unconscious level. Animals are a wonderful example. Research has proven time and again that when certain animals are isolated, they will carry out the functions necessary to sustain life. Examples of this would be squirrels storing nuts, and birds flying south for the winter. Intuition is the small voice inside that gives you a clear channel of communication that assists you in any endeavor.

Intuition can exist only in the development of oneself, which is accomplished by self examination. Edmund Shaftebury wrote on the subject of intuition, "The start is made when we understand that intuition is knowing a thing by direct information which springs out of the mind behind the brain. The information comes with a suddenness that is sometimes surprising, and it tells the truth so directly that it seems as if a higher power has sent it to the individual."

Intuition is much like instinct in the sense that in a new or different experience, one will respond to that event in the correct way. Nonetheless, intuition does so without knowledge, without experience, and without the thought process. Use your intuition in life; it is another one of your marvelous gifts. But you must set aside some quiet times to hear the small voice that is waiting to help you.

"L" is for leadership. Having leadership skills will strengthen your position with your clients and in your company. The by-product of leadership skills will position you to be a leader in your particular industry. It has been said that leadership is another word for courage. Leadership is the risk taking and the acceptance of responsibility. Leadership develops your communication skills, as well as your personal power in all your dealings.

As in the selling profession, leaders are not born, they are developed. Unfortunately, in this day and age leaders are a rare breed of people. The biggest reason for the lack of people assuming leadership roles is time.

Remember the words of a failure, "I don't have the time." Time devoted to leadership is an investment in the most important asset you have: yourself. Make time. There is more of it than you realize when you plan it.

"E" stands for enthusiasm. When you develop enthusiasm you will find that you have more energy, and you will feel happier, even if you feel like you are tired of your job. Act as if it is the greatest job in the world. The amazing truth is that by reciting that thought mentally, and acting as though it is true, it actually starts to be a great job. (I applied that philosophy when I worked on my grandfather's ranch shoveling fertilizer.) Enthusiasm starts with interest in the subject. When acquiring interest, you seek knowledge about the subject, which leads to the final stage of enthusiasm, belief. It would be safe to say that the more interest you have, the more knowledge you gain; the more knowledge you gain, the more belief you will have. This will generate an abundance of enthusiasm for the subject at hand. Make it a point with every prospect you meet to gauge their tempo-rhythm. It is your responsibility to match their tempo. You will be surprised how quickly they will relax and listen to you. This will make the entire presentation more successful and more enjoyable.

Adaptation

Stanislavski said, "Adaptation means both inner and outer means that people use in adjusting themselves to one another in a variety of relationships and also as an aid in affecting an object (person)."

- Constantin Stanislavski

It is important to realize that the adaptation process is comprised of three parts. The first is the assessment of the situation, followed by the selection of the type of adaptation to be used. Last is the carrying out of the adaptation. In your selling situation, you host a variety of emotions that you try to express to your prospect. In order to accomplish this, it is important that an intangible adaption take place. Adaptation should be to a sales person as salt is to the ocean. Adaptation mentally communicates to the prospect, "I am here for you, exclusively for you. In fact, I am willing to conform both in body position and in speech to build a rapport with you." Stanislavski believed in the power of adaptation. In fact, he included it in his elements of physical actions.

An adaptation has been defined as the overcoming of a physical obstacle in achieving your objective. When you fully understand your objective and have studied your prospect, adaptation will become second nature. Adaptation is the ability to respond to a given set of circumstances in a favorable matter.

Why is this important to a sales person? First, the sales person must conform to the prospect in a number of ways to be effective. If there is too much difference between them, then no real communication will take place in that interaction. By real communication, I mean communication that responds and is accepted by the other party. We can all talk at each other and try to convince, but that is not communicating. You must create affinity with the prospect to set the tone for open communication. The prospect must first like and relate to you before you can expect his or her to respond to you. This discussion does not refer to the physical appearance, although that does play a part in the relating stage. The issue here is whether you are relating to your prospect. Someone might ask, "Why doesn't the prospect relate to me?" You are the one who wants to persuade the individual, not the contrary. So, with that in mind, you must go about adapting to your prospect. Stanislavski taught that adaptation is essential in communication between actors on the stage. Selling is no different. You must present yourself on your prospect's level by building personal rapport.

In selling, you should constantly adapt yourself to the ever-changing climax of your presentation. Think about your body adapting. When chilled, your skin gets "goose pimples." This helps warm your body. When a bright light shines into your eyes, the pupils constrict. In times of extreme emergencies, your adrenalin glands will produce the necessary strength you need to overcome the circumstances. So, mentally we must adapt to be a more effective sales person.

Sonia Moore, one of Stanislavski's students in Russia, wrote, "New conditions of life, a new atmosphere, a new place the time of day or night all require appropriate adaptation. People behave differently at night than during the day. In a foreign country, one adjusts oneself to local conditions. The quality and variety of adaptation are extremely important on stage. To be interesting, an adaptation must be imaginative, in good taste, strong and sharp."

Affinity Revisited

Adaptation means, in many cases, the ability to create affinity with the prospect. Affinity is defined as the alikeness or oneness with something or someone. In selling, it is critical for the sales professional to create affinity as soon as possible. This could be having a mutual friend, or a similar experience. When you create that sameness, you will develop a rapport with the person you are trying to persuade.

It has been said that someone will form 12 opinions about you in seven seconds. If this is true, it is conceivable that you can analyze your prospect in that same span of time. In creating affinity with others, it is important to understand that all people have different social styles, so learning the different social styles of others will improve your ability to adapt to your prospects.

Wilson Learning Corporation designed a unique model for identifying social styles. The interesting part of this project is that everyone you meet will fall into one of these categories. First, let's discover your social style: Here is a condensed version.

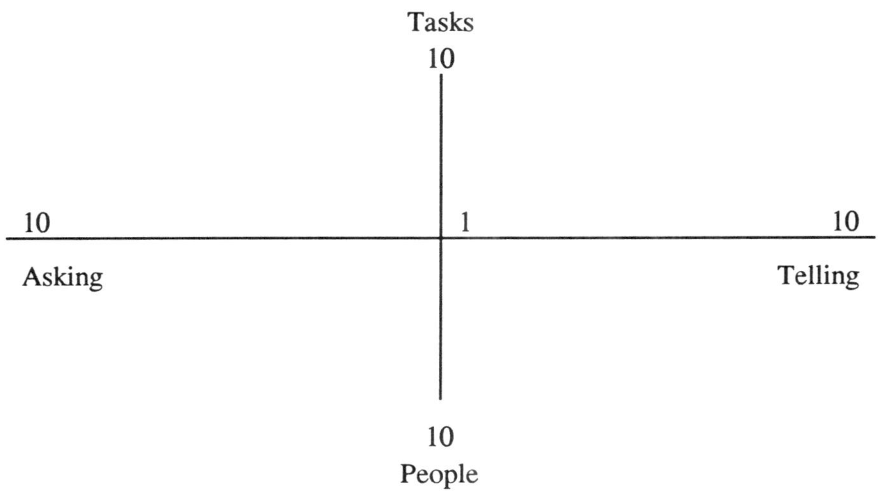

Rate yourself on a scale from one to ten, ten being on the top or bottom of the line. Ask yourself, do I do more asking or telling in my interactions with others? Then, proceed to rate yourself. Secondly, do I prefer performing tasks or dealing with people? Rate yourself from one to ten.

Now draw a line from your point on the line and connect it with your second point. You will discover your dominant social style. What is your social style?

Analytical	Driver
Amiable	Expressive

After you have discovered your social style, take a few minutes to figure out what the social style is for your parents, wife or husband, girlfriend or boyfriend, manager, co-workers. Now think about the social style of your top clients. Go back in your memory banks and think about a prospect who didn't buy from you. What was that person's social style? Knowing the little bit of information I have shared with you concerning this subject, what would you do differently in your presentation?

Here are some things to look for to identify the social style of your prospects. In addition, you will find their motivations, which will help you adapt your presentation to their mode of learning:

Social Style	Motivation	Adjectives
Analytical	Are interested in the process of your product.	Enterprising Methodical Persistent
Driver	Are interested in the bottom line. They want you to get to the point.	Obstinate Competent Definite
Amiable	Are interested in relationships and how things interact.	Understanding Reliable Agreeable
Expressive	Are interested in the vision and people and their activities.	Outgoing Emotional Spirited

Another unique way to create physical affinity is to mirror your prospect's body position. It is amazing how you will relax your prospects by mirroring their posture. The same applies to gestures they use while speaking to you. If, for example, they wave their arms while communicating their thoughts, and you do the same, you will find that their attention will be stronger because they will relate better to you.

Stanislavski concluded that adaptation is part of the actor's creative work. In addition, actors without an abundance of emotional capacity could provide more convincing performances through their ability to use adaptation. You must master this element of physical action to work in harmony in all your situations.

There are many different types of people you work with every day of your life, from the blue-collar worker to the high-level executive. Your adaptation, with practice, must be made consciously and, with time, unconsciously.

Make yourself adaptable and responsible to your prospect and watch the production report adapt to your new style of selling.

Introduction to Comic Book

"Children are not only our future, They are us!"

- JMR

In the artistic view, I thought it would be unique to share with you a comic book which illustrates the principles of selling. It would benefit society to look through the eyes of a child in our daily journey through life.

A story that best illustrates this point of view is that of a ten-year-old boy who was riding home after playing with his friends and came upon a group of people gathered around an 18-wheel truck that was apparently stuck in an underpass. There were wreckers and police officers gathered around to try to dislodge the huge vehicle. One of the officers told the boy that he would have to wait before he could proceed home.

The boy looked down and said, "Why don't they just let the air out of the tires?" The police officer looked down at all of the grown men struggling to pull the truck from the underpass. He went down and told them about the young boy's recommendation, which was implemented, and, of course, was successful. It would be wise to view selling from the eyes of a child. In this particular story, let's name this child Joey. Joey is the star of a comic book which will give you an excellent flavor of what selling is all about. The story is entitled, *Daddy, I Want to Be a Salesman*.

In my many years of selling, there were always the times when I, for whatever reason, had to schedule a nightly meeting in the home of the prospect. Think for a moment. You are seated at the kitchen table with your sales material, trying to get your points across, when a cute but interrupting child is competing for the attention of the prospect. Every time the attention of the parent is broken, you need to retrace your thoughts, so that they will appear in a logical sequence. In those times, you need a sales aid that will occupy the child and give you the quality time that you need to get you job done.

The comic coloring book entitled, *Daddy, I Wanna Be a Salesman*, is the answer. Children love new things, especially pictures, and the coloring book will describe for them the advantages of being a sales person.

The more we educate our children about the benefits of the sales person, the more we will help improve the image of the sales profession in the world in which we live. It is my firm belief that anyone entering the job market must gain the tremendous benefit of sales training. Many young college graduates are disappointed to find, after four long and stressful years at a leading university a soft job market.

Many individuals are waiting tables or working in jobs for which they are clearly over qualified simply because they are limiting themselves to the area of their degree.

There is no better way for someone to break into a corporation than in the sales field. You are able to learn more about a company, develop more as an individual, and reap tremendous rewards in a relatively short period of time by entering in the sales department than any other area of the company.

Many great company presidents started in sales. Sales is not just a department, it is a philosophy of life. Words like service, dedication, valued added, and responsibility describe the sales profession.

Daddy I Want to Be a Salesman...

by James M. Rankin

Illustrations by Michael Janota

The school bell rang out and all the kids began pouring out of the classroom, into the hallway, and then out the door to the street.

Joey, Robert and Susan, who were all good friends, were walking home together.

Susan said, “Did you hear about the fire last night?”

"Yes," said Robert, in a quiet voice.

Susan went on. "The house was damaged pretty bad. Luckily, no one was hurt, but the whole upstairs was ruined."

Joey asked, "How do you know so much about the fire?"

"Well, my daddy is a fireman," she said proudly. "Did you know the fire was started by a couple of kids playing with matches? Doesn't everyone know that matches are nothing but trouble?"

"I don't want to hurt my family or ruin my house with those silly things," Joey said.

Susan asked, “Robert, what does your dad do for a living?”

“He is a scientist. He’s been a scientist for about ten years,” Robert said.

Susan asked Joey the same question.

Joey stopped and said, "I don't know what my dad does."

Joey walks in the door to his home.
"Mom, I'm home!" yelled Joey.
"Joey, get started on your homework so you can have the rest of the day to play."

"Mom, what does Dad do for a living?" asked Joey.

"Your father is a salesman," said Mother.

"A salesman, Dad is a salesman!" Joey said with a surprised look on his face.

Joey and his father, after dinner, went into the den to talk. Joey knows that talking to his parents is very important, even if his parents forget to do it.

Joey asked his father, "Dad, what is a salesman?"

"A salesman is one of the most important parts of our economy."

"The economy is the buying and selling of everything from your toys to hot dogs, to cars. Salesmen keep the businesses open in our country."

"When someone learns and masters the selling profession, they will always have a job."

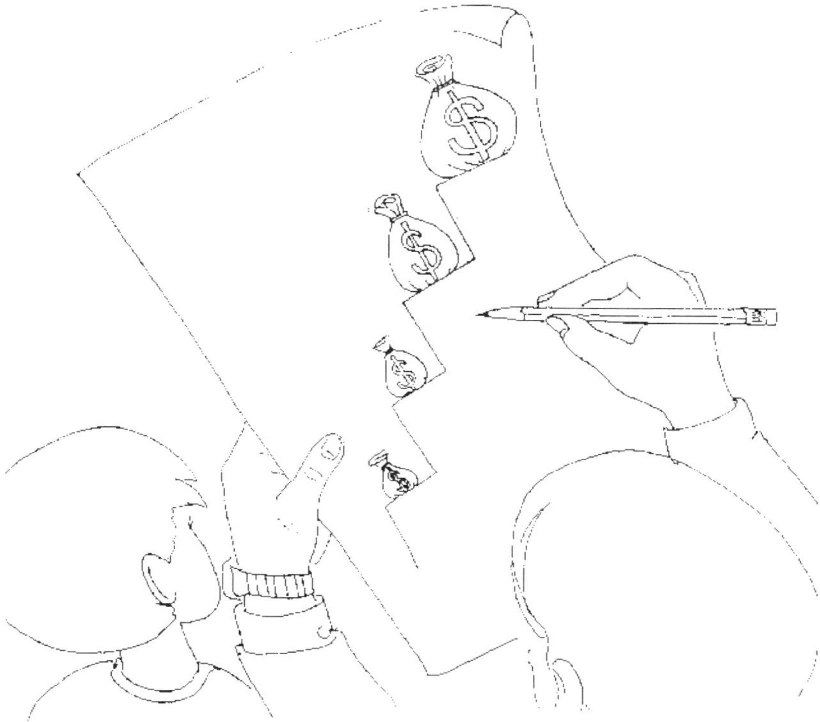

"Every company in the world needs professional salespeople. The money that they earn is based on what the person wants to earn. You could compare it to steps. Let me show you."

+ $75,000 - Unlimited
+ $25,000 - $75,000
+ $10,000 - $25,000
poverty

"You and you alone determine which step you want to be on, and what step you end up on."

"Dad, I want to be a salesman!" Joey said excitedly.

"It is never too early to start learning the principles of being a good salesman," said his father. "The first part of being a top salesman is having a good self image."

Joey asked, "What do you mean by self image?" "Self image is how you see yourself through your own eyes, how you feel about who you are," his dad said.

"Who am I, Dad?" Joey asked his dad.

"Son, you are many things to many people. For example, you are my son."

"You are Grandma's grandson."

"You are Robert's friend."

"You are Coach Campbell's second baseman."
"You have many roles that you play."

"You are a boy who is smart and who can be trusted. You have a lot of value. For you see, there has never been anyone in the world that is just like you. That makes you valuable"

"Am I really that valuable?" asked Joey.

"You better believe you are!" his dad answered. "Remember that you must believe you are valuable. You must first like yourself before others can like you. Joey, do you like Joey?"

"I think I do. Yes, I like me a lot!" replied Joey.

"Joey, the next step in becoming a good salesman is that you must like people. You see, a salesman doesn't just sell things like shoes, houses or cars. A good salesman sells the benefits the individual will receive from owning what it is he is selling."

"He must do that in a friendly way. The key here is not to act friendly, rather to be friendly. Products are what salesmen sell to the public. A product would be your bike, clothes, even your baseball mitt."

"How do I know what the benefits are for someone, Dad?" asked Joey.

"Product knowledge is knowing, as well as your name, all of the things that the product will do. But, more important, product knowledge is showing your client how the product will improve his life. Put another way, you don't sell what the product is, rather you sell what it does for the client," said Joey's father.

"That," Joey said, "sounds like fun. I would like to help people. Why doesn't everyone want to be a salesman?"

"There are a lot of jobs that help people. Selling is one of them. Selling is not for everyone."

"If you like to meet people and help people solve problems, if you like to travel and never do the same thing every day, then selling is for you," replied Dad.

Little sister Jill, walked into the room and said, "Daddy, I want to watch TV."

"Honey, in a minute," Dad said. "If you want to get ahead, stop watching so much TV every day and start reading good books."

"So salesmen sell benefits not products. Oh, Dad, can girls be salesmen?"

"Girls sure can be in the profession of selling; in fact, remember Mrs. Carlson?"

"Yes," Joey said, "she showed us this house."

"She showed us the benefit of living in this house and now we live here," Joey's dad replied.

"I remember she sure asked a lot of questions, didn't she, Dad."

"I seem to remember that she did. Questions are very important in selling. That is the way to find out how someone feels about something; never stop asking questions. If you want to know something, always ask. You are a problem solver."

"Just like in my math class. You mean like solving for 8 + 4 = 12, Dad?"

"That is correct. But, bring along your six wise men who will teach you everything you need to know. Those wise men are Who, What, When, Where, Why, and How."

"So, there is more to listening than just hearing," said Joey.

Dad said, "Hearing is physical, listening is mental."

"This is real interesting. The stuff we are talking about can benefit everyone, not just the salesman, right?" Joey asked.

"Joey, everyone is a salesperson, whether he knows it or not. It's just that some lucky people get a paycheck from doing it."

"The next principle is a little known secret that I learned early in life. The secret is goal setting," explained Joey's father.

"Goal setting?" Joey asked.

"You watch football on TV, and have seen the goal post on the field, haven't you?"

"Those players are heading down the field to score the touchdown. They have direction and that means they know where they are going. We all need to know where we are going if we want to score in the game of life. The way to do that is by setting goals."

"Goals are what I want to do," Joey said.
"That is correct. Goals are what you want to do now and in the future."

"There are some important points about goal setting. There are the three "P's" when talking about goal setting. The first "P" stands for personal. Joey, state your goal using the word "I."

"I want to make the majors in the little league."

"That is a goal. State it personally. The next "P" is to write it in the present time. Try that, Joey."

"I am in the major league."

"Write down what you want in a positive way. Joey, you did that in your goal."

"You mean to write what I want, not what I don't want?"

"You are right again. Goal setting is very important in your future plans, or your daily plans. Write what you want on a piece of paper using the ideas we have talked about earlier. Put a time deadline on each goal."

"So I won't put off the things I want, Dad?"

"Right," said Joey's dad. "Live your life each day and make it so beautiful that when you think about it, it will bring a smile to your face. Plan your work, work your plan, but live your life moment to moment."

"Thanks, Dad. Good night," Joey said.

"Pleasant dreams! Super salesman!" said his father.

"Hey Susan, I found out what my dad does for a living," said Joey.

"Really? What does he do?" asked Susan.

"He is a salesman!" replied Joey excitedly.

"Wow, your dad is a salesman? What does he sell?"

"Oh, benefits. Yeah, he sells benefits!" Joey answered.

Someday, I am going to be a super salesman too!"

The Dedicated and Inspiring Life of a Sales Pro

In all the printed information on selling, it has yet to be discussed that selling is as natural as sleeping. Everyone buys and sells every day of their lives; starting from the breakfast at their neighborhood fast food restaurant, to the gas to run their cars, to the idea that they sold to their colleague on the job. We are all buyers and sellers. It is the foundation of our way of life.

In researching for this project, I found an unnamed book that discussed, in detail, taking a customer from no interest to a close. Why spend the time to develop interest in customers? Interest and desire are alike in the sense that it is difficult to create these traits in others. It can be done, and is accomplished every day. But for the professional sales person, the job is to find buyers. It makes the job easier and rewarding for you, as well as more beneficial for the client and the company.

A sales pro should develop a natural style of selling. In Method Selling, it is very important to let the elements become part of your sales personality. To execute the principles without conscious thought will prove to be a tremendous benefit to you. Many sales people feel that spontaneity is critical to their presentation. They feel that if they concentrate on the method, they will lose that part of themselves in the business of selling. Stanislavski said, "In every branch of art, as well as in music, the work and preparation ruled by discipline should finally disappear, so that the elegance and freshness for the form should strike us as being spontaneous."

Selling and marketing go together like Butch Cassidy and the Sundance Kid. Marketing and selling are both consumer oriented. The two critical steps of both are, first, to address and identify the needs of the prospect, and second, to fill those needs with a particular product or service. The sales person is a dedicated individual who uses inspiration in every phase of his or her professional life.

"The Life of a Sales Pro," unlike the story of "The Death of a Salesman," is an essay of inspiration, or spirit, and determination. It is not an easy life; in fact, it can be quite lonely. The willingness to serve is often shattered with negative thoughts and actions. The desire to help solve a problem is met with a cold, "I'm not interested." The innermost part of yourself cries out to help the human condition, and is met with indifference.

Yet, the unknown soldiers march on in spite of society's callous attitude toward sales people. What drives them to continue to pick themselves up after letdowns, disappointments and outright hostility? Why? Thousands of individuals ask themselves that and eventually get out of the business of selling. There is a saying that I grew up with that states, "Winners never quit, and quitters never win." Those words are powerful when they are mentally digested.

Many people may be puzzled by the words mentally digested. However, I believe wholeheartedly the words of my grandfather, who said, "If I would feed my mind as much as I did my stomach, then I would never have to worry about my stomach, or a roof over my head, or money in the bank." Society has paid a lot of lip service to the concept of positive thinking, but has done little to ingrain its meaning into the hearts and minds of people. The laws of nature are simple: One, in particular, states that for every action, there is an equal and opposite reaction.

Another saying that I grew up with was, "Birds of a feather flock together." The meaning behind the saying is that thoughts seem to attract events and circumstances. Thoughts are real things and can bring to us what we desire.

Ella Wheeler Wilcox said that "Man is what he thinks, not what he says, reads or hears. By persistent thinking, you can undo any condition which exists. You can free yourself from any chains whether of poverty, sin, ill health, unhappiness or fear."

"The Life of a Sales Pro" is the story of you and me. Because, when it comes right down to it, we are all sales people. We try to sell our friends the idea that we are useful to them. Teachers sell their students on the value of an education. Businesses, regardless of the nature of their business, sell their customers on their service. Let me share a story that illustrates the importance of good salesmanship.

> *I'm your customer who never came back. I'm a nice customer. All merchants know me. I'm the one who never complains no matter what kind of service I get. When I go to a store to buy something, I don't throw my weight around. I try to be thoughtful of the other person.*
>
> *If I get a snotty clerk who gets nettled because I want to look at several things before I make up my mind, I'm as polite as can be. I don't believe rudeness in return is the answer. I never kick, complain or criticize, and I wouldn't dream of making a scene, as I have seen people doing in public places.*
>
> *No, I'm a nice customer, but I'm the nice customer who never came back. That's my little revenge for being abused, and taking whatever you hand out, because I know I'm not coming back. That way doesn't immediately relieve my feelings, but in the long run it's far more satisfying than blowing my top.*
>
> *In fact, a nice customer like myself multiplied by others of my kind can ruin a business, and there are a lot of nice people just like me. When we get pushed far enough, we go to another store where they appreciate nice customers.*

He laughs best, they say, who laughs last. I laugh when I see you frantically advertising to get me back when you could have kept me in the first place with a few kind words and a smile. Your business might be in different towns, and your situation might be "different." But if business is bad, chances are good that if you change your attitude, the word will get around.

I will change from one nice customer who never came back to the nice customer who always comes back and brings his friends.

- Anonymous -

In the profession of selling there emerges, in the eyes of certain people, the image of the fast talking man wearing his plaid jacket and promising you the world. He is selling the end result of the sale for him, not you.

We are very fortunate to have had some great sales trainers such as Dale Carnegie, Tom Hopkins, Earl Nightingale and Zig Ziglar. These men have decided to use their talents and abilities to train other salespeople instead of getting rich in their chosen profession. They have enriched the lives of their salespeople, who enrich the lives of their clients, which helps our whole economic system.

"The Life of a Sales Pro" can greatly enrich your life if you are dealing with a professional sales pro. The first rule of selling is qualifying. When a sales professional calls on you, then you qualify for the benefits they are selling.

In this day and age, with such a rapidly expanding source of information, it is important to keep abreast of new ideas and concepts that can greatly improve your lifestyle. What better way to understand these ideas than with an informed, empathetic sales person who sincerely is looking out for your interest.

In the life of a Sales Pro they sometimes run across a prospect who is downright rude, indicated by either a hang-up on the phone, a slammed door, or an escort from the premises. Those may be extreme, but I am trying to dramatize the rejection that occurs in the marketplace.

First of all, we must realize that just as you do your job, a Sales Pro is doing his or her job. The Sales Pro's job is just as important as yours. This doesn't mean that you have to stop everything to hear their story, but a little human kindness is in order. It doesn't take a lot of energy to say, "No, thank you, or I've got my bases covered on that product, but thanks all the same."

You know that when you do that, you make that sales person feel better because, after all, you are talking with a real person with real feelings. All people should be treated with respect. You will find that you will feel better, too.

We find that prospects who have been upset by a pushy sales person will project that attitude from the event to every sales person who walks into that person's life. Sell the way you like to buy.

This reminds me of the story of the wind and the sun. They were arguing whether they could make this guy take off his jacket. The wind went first and tried to blow the jacket off of him. The harder the wind blew the tighter, the guy held on to his jacket. The wind gave up, so the sun slowly beamed down its rays and after a few minutes the guy just slipped off his jacket.

The Chinese are known for their poetic philosophy of life. Some of my favorites are: the journey of a thousand miles starts with a single step, or the flowers of tomorrow are in the seeds of today. These are examples of action. We live in a society where procrastination comes naturally. It has been said that 80 percent of all decisions can be made immediately. We must act to be effective.

Here is a poem that says it so well:

When I was hungry, you formed a humanitarian club to discuss my hunger.

Thank you.

I was imprisoned and you crept off quietly to your chapel in the cellar and prayed for my release.

I was naked and in your mind you debated the morality of my appearance.

I was sick and you knelt and thanked God for your health.

I was homeless and you preached to me of the spiritual shelter of the love of God.

I was lonely and you left me alone to pray for me.

You seem so holy; so close to God.

But I'm still very hungry and lonely and cold.

So where have your prayers gone?

What have they done?

What does it profit a man to page through his book of prayers when the rest of the world is crying for help?

- The Churchman, Diocese of Dallas

The point is, ideas are good, prayers are even better; however, if not taken in by action they are lifeless. Remember, God helps those who help themselves. Action should be embedded in the life pattern of all people. Zig Ziglar said it so well when he said, "When you sow an action, you reap a habit. When you sow a habit, you reap a character. When you sow a character, you reap a destiny."

We all must be activated. When we are activated, our alertness is keen, our mind is sharp, our production is greatly increased. In *The Life of a Salesman*, action is the word of the day. Og Mandino wrote in his book, *The Greatest Salesman in the World,* "My dreams are worthless, my plans are dust, my goals are impossible. All are of no value unless they are followed by action."

We need to take charge of our lives, for you see, we control our thoughts. Our thoughts control our feelings, and our feelings control our actions. William James, the Father of Psychology, also teaches us that action triggers feeling and feelings trigger action. In other words, to be a person of action, you must think action.

The Process of the Sale

Method sellers know that selling is a process. Every basic selling course describes the different stages you go through in the course of your presentation. Let's review the steps and redefine the total process so it flows in a logical sequence. For many of you, this will be a review; however, you may pick up additional insights which will ensure your success in working with your prospects. The stages are: introduction, probing, presentation, documentation, compromising, and the completion stage.

Introduction Stage

Reviewing your past successes, you will find that your introduction stage was executed thoroughly. You left your briefcase closed, your rate book stayed on your lap and your focus was on your prospect. When you meet a prospect who has been referred by someone that the prospect holds in high esteem, your job will be so much easier. Look at your sales records and you will discover a higher percentage of sales were to referred leads. The secret behind a referred lead is that you are able to ride on the existing relationship of the friend or associate. You are suddenly a team mate on the conference winning high school football team or the neighbor at the family picnic or you are in that freshman class of incoming junior executives. The power of the referred lead will allow you to connect to your new prospect in the most efficient way. An important point to remember is that the spotlight is on your prospects. Give them your full attention and try to get them to open up to you. If they are reluctant to open up to you in the introduction stage, you will be starting at a disadvantage. It is possible, however, to win them over in the course of the sales presentation, but the key is to take your time in the introduction stage. Take a sincere interest in your prospects. Dale Carnegie wrote in his classic book *Winning Friends and Influencing People*, "you can make more friends in two months taking an interest in others than you can in two years trying to get people interested in you."

Another important point, don't miss the opportunity to ask for referrals from people who don't buy or who don't make appointments with you. This will make cold calling a more productive activity. Follow each step and don't bypass a step; otherwise you will short-circuit the entire process. Many sales people tell me, "I'm just not a people person." Take just a few minutes to write down the names of people whom you know who are warm, friendly, and fun to be around and list some their characteristics. You have the ability to develop those traits and use them every day of your life.

Probing Stage

The next step is the probing stage. Probing extends beyond mere superficial question asking. Probing is taking a deep empathetic view into the interworkings of the company and the individual you are working with in the course of your activities. Probing has been defined as "investigating thoroughly" by Webster's dictionary.

Let's establish a few basics in terms of the probing stage. Always ask in the initial stage broad-based questions such as: the nature of the business, years in service. You will then proceed into more specific areas such as what the company is using now instead of your product offering and how they feel about it. What improvements can they foresee in this area? Don't make the mistake of a "twenty question" game. This makes people feel very uncomfortable and prevents any possibility of forming a relationship. The key to effective probing is to piggyback on the previous answer. This is not only a good interviewing skill, but it shows your prospects you are listening to what they are saying in the exchange. Paraphrasing is a very important skill to learn. It is simply restating what your prospect has just communicated to you. The benefit of paraphrasing is that it allows your prospect to hear what they were trying to say to you. They now have a chance to correct, clarify or restate their views. Also, you will want to ask open ended questions.

Open ended questions are questions that cannot be answered with a yes or no. Example: What is important to you in your health insurance program? This question prompts your prospect to talk to you. Closed questions, on the other hand, require only a yes or a no answer. They are used when you need to obtain information quickly.

Watch the professional interviewers such as Mike Wallace of Sixty Minutes, Larry King of Larry King Live. They both have the ability to get people to open up. Although, they have two entirely different styles, they both get results. You have your own unique style which can be used to extract information from your prospects-information that can help you better understand the prospect's situation from the prospect's point of view.

Presentation Stage

Presentation stage is when the spotlight is on you. You are on stage and you have been given the cue. You are now ready to bring the solutions to your prospect's problems to life in your product offering. (The cue will be given to you by your prospect.) Sales professionals know that after the probing stage they have a qualified prospect. Think of yourself as a professional baseball player at the plate. They don't swing at every pitch, and contrary to popular beliefs, you don't go through a complete presentation to someone who will not make the final decision or who is not qualified to be a client. Why go through the fruitless motion? How many times have you performed your presentation to someone you knew wouldn't buy it? How did you feel?

It is awkward for you and your prospect in this situation. You should have a condensed version to share the essence of what you do with others; however, you would not go through an entire presentation with someone who cannot make a decision. It is true in working with large corporations that there are people who are paid to listen to you and there are committees to work through; however, don't forget to ask in the probing stage who will make the final decision.

Here are a few points to keep in mind when you are performing a presentation:

- Are you dressed appropriately?
- Do you have adequate eye contact with your prospect?
- Is there sufficient time spent in the different stages?
- Rate yourself in your performance of these stages:

Introduction stage?	Need improvement 1 2 3 4 5 Excellent
Probing stage?	Need improvement 1 2 3 4 5 Excellent
Presentation?	Need improvement 1 2 3 4 5 Excellent
Documentation?	Need improvement 1 2 3 4 5 Excellent
Compromising stage?	Need improvement 1 2 3 4 5 Excellent
Completion stage?	Need improvement 1 2 3 4 5 Excellent

- Does your voice reflect warmth and friendliness?
- Is there voice inflection?
- Do you use pauses effectively?
- Are you using hand gestures to communicate your thoughts?
- Is your voice strong and distinct?
- Does the tempo-rhythm of the presenter match the client?
- Does the presenter match the speech sense of the client?
- Is the super objective communicated effectively?
- What does the body-language of the presenter communicate to the client?
- Are the props used effectively in the presentation?
- Is there two-way communication between the presenter and the client?
- Is a referral presentation given to the client?
- Is value added service included in the sales script?
- Are you relaxed and well informed?

Documentation Stage

Just how convincing are you? No matter how articulate you may be, there is a question in the mind of most your prospects: "Who besides you says that your product is good?" The best example for sales professionals is the law profession. When an attorney enters the courtroom, what does he or she bring into the courtroom? If you were a juror and the attorney just showed up and said, "Please let my client go, he is innocent, " how would you respond? Put yourself in your prospect's shoes. You need to equip yourself with third party endorsements for your products and articles stating the benefits of the concepts of your offering. Back up your ideas with facts that are proven and withstand the litmus test of truth. Secondly, have letters from clients who are benefiting from your program. This will not only convince your prospects, but will strengthen your relationship with the client. Volunteer to write the letter if your client expresses doubt about the ability to write it. It is also effective to have support information when objections arise in the sales process. A true life example is the price objection. I had a letter from a client that stated, "I was reluctant at first to invest in the program because of the perceived costs. However, after using the program it has paid for itself ten times over." The documentation stage will help make your meetings convincing, persuasive and more effective. Get the support of your sales associates to gather additional letter; and pass them out to everyone.

Comprising Stages

The compromising stage is a very important part of the total sales process. This is a stage where you listen to and address concerns that your prospect may have concerning your product or service. Please remember this simple bit of wisdom. Objections show interest, whereas, no questions, no interest. The misconception of many sales professionals is that when a prospect objects, you need to attack and defend your presentation. Nothing could be further from the truth. The secret is to listen attentively and actively to your prospect and get as much information as you can about the objection. Here's a dynamic question. "Mrs. Rogers, is there anything else that would prevent you from owning this program?" She replies, "No". You now are in a great position to complete the sale. If you can answer her objection to her utmost satisfaction, you will have a new client. Remember you are paid more for asking the right questions than knowing the right answers. Use the most important word in our language to uncover feeling: Why?

Roger Fisher and William Ury wrote an interesting book called *Getting to Yes*. In the book, they outlined the steps to effectively reach decisions with others. The first part is to separate the people from the problem. Too many times, personalities get in the way of reaching an agreement. Compromise is not giving in to others wishes or having them give into yours. Compromise has been defined by Webster's Dictionary as: "something midway." Compromising is coming to a reasonable, fair agreement between two parties. In any negotiations there will be give and take between individuals, and the same applies in your sales situation. You must be willing to work with your prospect.

The prospect that you are working with needs to be viewed first as a human being and not just as a sale. As in all exchanges, there are two vital elements: First is the product you are marketing and second is the relationship between you and your prospect. This part of the process encompasses perception, emotion, communicating and prevention.

The key is to listen carefully to your prospect's concerns and recognize the emotions. Stephen Covey wrote in his book, *The Seven Effective Habits of Successful People*, "Seek first to understand, then to be understood." The objection you receive from your prospect should be addressed and not the person expressing these concerns.

Focus on your prospect's interest and not the positions the prospect is taking in the process. As Mr. Fisher and Mr. Ury point out, the interest of your prospects will define the underlying objectives. It's interesting to discover that there are compatible, mutually shared interests behind opposed positions. The only way to find out your prospect's interests is the probing stage.

When you are brainstorming with your prospects, you will invent options for mutual gain. The story of the brothers arguing over the last apple is a classic. They both expressed how much they needed the apple. Their father did the logical thing and split the apple into two halves. One brother ate the apple and threw away the seeds, and the other brother threw away the apple and kept the seeds. Communicate with your prospects and you will find very similar situations. It's important to have an objective standard to confirm your claims. In real estate, you have market comparisons and the same set of criteria exists in every industry.

Lastly, is what the authors coined as a BATNA. This is an acronym for Best Alternative to a Negotiated Agreement. Bottom line is that no one sale is going to define who you are in your life. Don't bank everything you are on a single presentation. You will lose your objectivity and your competitive edge. You need to develop other alternatives to your marketing plan should the sale not materialize.

Completion Stage

What is in a name? Everything! Name recognition is a secret ingredient for the success of many large corporations. Name recognition is a valuable commodity. A name can radiate quality and value. Why am I using completion instead of the "C" word?. The word *close* is so final and it implies a type of hit and run mentality. It is important not to fragment your presentation.

Have you ever been in a presentation and you suddenly realize it is time to close? You hesitate, your prospect is waiting to hear the words. You stutter and manage to say, "Well, what would you like to do?" Actors learn and study their lines, so it is only logical that you learn your concluding lines and incorporate them throughout your presentation. This can be referred to as trial completion questions.

The minute you walk in the door, you should be expecting and executing the perceived reality that this prospect will be your client. I remember in my early days of selling, I couldn't wait to use new ideas in my presentation. I loved the "ownership strategy." It was so powerful, yet so subtle. I would tell the prospect, "When you receive your policy, your name will go here." You are planting seeds which will rapidly grow when you bring your presentation to life.

Don't subscribe to the argument that you are trying to trick your prospect into buying. You are using the most effective tools to bring your prospect into your family of clients. The sales presentation is a process and the completion stage is consummating the transaction. Get your paperwork completed. The prospect will sense if you are nervous about asking for this sale. If you are hesitating about the program, why should they feel good about it? Right! You must have confidence and provide reassurance to the prospect that this is indeed a good decision. The fundamentals of securing a sale involve talking to qualified prospects. Do your homework in prospecting for clients. Get feedback from your prospects throughout the presentation: "Can you see how this would help you?"

You see, the major decision is really all the minor agreements that you obtain throughout your presentation.

In the compromising stage, when you hear the objection, try a trial completion question. "Are there any other concerns you may have which would prevent you from owning the program?"

An important detail that cripples more sales careers and even ends many promising careers is the reluctance of the sales professional to ask for the order. When you follow the stages which I have just outlined, you will increase your sales production tenfold.

There are several common mistakes I have observed in working with sales people. One obvious mistake is not pre-qualifying your prospect. How do you per-qualify your prospects? The answer is found in the prospecting process when you ask the right questions. If the individual is hard to handle on the telephone, chances are great that you will have difficulty in a sales situation. Ask important, pertinent questions to ensure that the prospect is as excited about seeing you as you are to see him or her.

Lack of knowledge is like building your house on shifting sand. Your sales career should be built on your knowledge of the product, your company, your prospect and your ability to relate to others. How many times has a prospect asked you questions that you didn't have the answer to? There are those individuals who will tell you that you don't need to have all the answers. You certainly don't want to guess at your answers, yet a sale is postponed until you obtain the information. Anticipate questions and research the answers so you are prepared to play your role. Think and act like the professional sales person you are.

Another spoiler is trying to get too much feedback, which is just delaying asking for the order. For example, "What do you like about the program? Oh, really! Why is that important to you? What else?

And why is that important to you? And on, and on, and on Get their okay on the paperwork, they are ready to buy! When you see the buying signs and you hear the words, complete the transaction. You will have time to build a relationship with your new client as soon as you get the product or service implemented.

On the other hand, don't be too aggressive. Has anyone ever walked up to you in a clothing store or a car dealership and said, "What will it take to get your business today?" That's the introductory line? Does a person who cares about your needs and concerns make statements like that? I don't think so. A hard fact to understand is that people want to do business with people that don't necessarily need the business.

Put another way, people don't want to work with someone who seems desperate to get the sale. The logic is simple; if you are struggling in your business you won't be around to service your client. Remember the "magic if" and the "act as if" principles in Method Selling. This will allow you to project the right temperament and image to your prospects.

Don't fall into the trap of using cookie cutter closes. Listen carefully, you need to learn a structured closing script; however, there are different closes for different individuals. For some of your prospects who are candidates, but are stalling making the decision, you could make a statement to the effect, "You'll always be glad you made this decision. What is your social security number?" Other individuals will not respond to this type of close. The point here is to fit the close to the social style of your prospect and don't be afraid to go with your intuition. Free yourself from fear, so you can discover the best strategy to obtain the sale. Top professionals love this part of the business because it is challenging and rewarding. You don't necessarily have to have a hundred closing scripts, but you do need a variety.

People, by their very nature, will procrastinate making a decision. Your mission is to assist individuals in making decisions. Another example I have used with prospects in the completion stage is the three legged stool example. Everyone needs to be fair to the rest of the team, I would tell the prospect.

The stool has three legs; the first leg is the client, second is the company, and lastly the sales professional. You, as the client, have to get a fair shake, so you feel good about the program. The company has to do its part so it can back up the product and service and can continue to produce the end product. The sales professional has to be treated fairly so he or she can maintain the service to the market place.

This is what is referred to as a win/win/win relationship. If any of the legs are not present or are weakened because of the transaction, the stool will not stand. Stephen Covey, in his classic book, *The Seven Habits of Highly Effective People*, discusses the win/win philosophy.

> "Win/Win is a frame of mind and heart that constantly seeks mutual benefit in all human interactions. Win/Win means that agreements or solutions are mutually beneficial, mutually satisfying. With a Win/Win solution, all parties feel good about the decision and feel committed to the action plan. Win/Win sees life as a cooperative, not a competitive arena. Most people tend to think in terms of dichotomies: strong or weak, hardball or softball, win or lose. But that kind of thinking is fundamentally flawed. It's based on power and position rather than on principle. Win/Win is based on the paradigm that there is plenty for everybody, that one person's success is not achieved at the expense or exclusion of the success of others."

When your prospect buys from you, everybody wins. You have to take the bulk of the responsibility for the success of the process. Study the stages and don't be afraid to ask as many times as it takes to obtain the order. You are not being pushy or aggressive, you are simply doing your job. Remember the old saying, "It's not what you say, it's how you say it." It's been stated that asking the client five times is the magic number in the completion stage. I feel it's whatever number it takes to get the job done. The psychology behind the number is that if you are willing to hang in there with all the rejections, then your program must really be good. We call that belief in your program. Try asking for the order when the prospect says a flat out, "No." Who knows, they might just buy.

Your Presentation, Your Script

In our society we focus more on the training of what not to do versus what we should be doing. However, it is true that there are pitfalls we should be made aware of to prevent unnecessary mental anguish. In the creation of your role, you should have an idea of the sales professional you want to become. A polished, articulate, empathetic individual is a good image to focus on; one who is confident and secure in his or her abilities and has a strong desire to solve a prospect's problem.

When we walk in that door, and after the greeting, we should not waste our prospect's time by rattling on about something outside the content of the presentation. We have, much like an actor, a time frame and lines that must be communicated, so state your purpose for the meeting. Our presentation is similar to a play; it has a story line followed with introduction of the characters, rising action, comic relief, climax and conclusion, followed by signed applications.

Can you imagine an actor walking on stage without knowing his lines? It would be unthinkable, yet thousands of sale people every day go into meetings without all the facts, without a thorough knowledge of their product. In Method Selling, we discussed the super objective which will lead you back to the intention of your prospects i.e., protecting their home against fire, college education for their kids, a new computer system for the office. Ignoring the time clock can destroy your presentation. You must allow for questions and feedback. Another pitfall is talking to yourself. This means you are reciting a presentation word for word. Some sales people even have cue cards that they read to the prospect. Method sellers relate to their prospect in words and action. Taking responsibility for the prospect's understanding is accomplished by asking your prospects if they understood your last point, or if they see how the product could help them in a certain area. Let's not forget that selling and acting are similar in nature by virtue of the element of relating.

In acting, the character relates to the audience by the words of the playwright. Your audience is your prospect when you share the words of your sales script. Your job, as that of an actor, is to convince others as to your wishes and intentions. A script should be followed carefully, without deviation. Yet, you as a sales professional have the opportunity to mold your script to fill the needs of your client. You are able to personalize it to address a potential solution using your product. As in a good staged production, you need a powerful close. This is what will stand out the most in your prospect's mind. Dramatize your product's benefits in a story form. Bring life to your product by talking about others who have benefited from owning your product.

Your sales presentation is much like an actor's script. Here are a few tips to ensure that your presentation has the vital elements to be an effective sales script.

Sales Script Critique

1. Length of time of presentation.____________________

2. Does the script contain trial completion questions?__________

3. Does the presentation have support documentation which includes research, studies, etc.?____________________

4. Does the presentation have letters of recommendations from satisfied clients or endorsements from peers?__________

5. Does the presentation contain at least three questions that allow the client to answer in the affirmative?______________

6. Does the presentation contain probing questions dealing with the client's needs and wants?____________________

7. Does the presentation translate features into benefits?________

8. Does the presentation stimulate emotions?____________________

9. Are there living examples of people enjoying the end result of the product or service being offered to the client?__________________

10. Is the presentation thorough in its explanation of the company, products, or services?____________________________

11. Does the product presentation clearly illustrate that it is indeed the solution to the client's problem?__________________

12. Is there a referral presentation in the script?___________________

13. Is the mission of the company communicated to the client?_______

14. Does the sales script contain alternative closing questions?_______

15. Are the client's responses restated?__________________________

You will find that people will begin to relate to you, which means, more relationships and more sales if you incorporate these elements into your script.

Improving Your Stage Presence

The thoughts we continue to dwell on over the years are not mere dreams or fantasies. They become the blueprint with which we build the role we play in life. How we see ourselves reflects back to our audience. How do we improve our presence to attract and hold the attention of others? A good example of holding attention is the ocean waves. Do you ever get tired of the waves of the oceans as they rise and fall?

You are mesmerized by the waves for three very important reasons. The elements that comprise this powerful scene are color, sound and movement. The color of the water coupled with the sound of the waves as they crash on the white sands of the shoreline. The movement of the waves helps you focus on this marvel of nature. You have seen plays and movies where the director tries to portray a character as either rich or poor by using costumes. Think about it; when we take one character and change his clothes, we change our perception of that character. You control what you wear to a certain extent, so be conscious of this fact when you are creating your role.

Master Voice Inflection

The sound of your voice reflects the attitude in your mind. Actors train their voices because that is one of the most important tools they use in their craft. Sales people would do well to follow their example. Listen to your own voice carefully. Can you hear the intent? To change your voice, you must first change your thoughts. To sound warm and friendly, think warm and friendly thoughts. Voice inflection is taught in acting schools throughout the world. Voice inflection will capture the attention of your prospect. Controlling your voice enables you to control the sales climax of your presentation. Actors work hard on the inflection because they know that if they put too much stress on a word they will change the entire meaning of the sentence and the intent of the playwright. Let's look at an example.

Consider the sentence: I didn't say the boat was broken. If you emphasize the first word "I," the meaning of the sentence changes to mean someone else said it, but not me. If you stress "Didn't," this changes to a flat denial. If you stress the word "Say," it changes to mean I may have implied that but I didn't say it. "Boat," it was the car that was not working. Lastly, I didn't say the boat was "broken." Now it suddenly changes to mean it was banged up, but not broken. The point of the exercise is to sensitize you to the importance of emphasizing your words correctly.

Consciously stressing the critical word will reinforce your super objective. This will add clarity to your presentation, and influence your prospect. Your stage presence boils down to your own unique style. There is a lot of competition out there, so it is essential that we, first of all, set ourselves apart from the competition. You alone set your product apart either in a positive or negative way, by your style of communication. That personal touch of yours will build interest in your prospect. It is important to remember the first part of the sales process is to get the prospect to like and trust you. Although we all may have the same lines, we never say them the same way. Everyone incorporates their own style in repeating those words in their presentation. It is interesting that a sales force with the same sales script, same product, same economic condition in the marketplace produces different sales results. Why is that? Style is the answer, coupled with a solid sales strategy.

Watch the sales leaders in your organization and learn from them. You will notice that none of their styles are the same, yet they are working for those sales people because it is their own style. Develop your own unique sales style by directing your attention to your prospects and make them feel comfortable. You accomplish this by creating in your sales presentation what Stanislavski called the "Ego of the Role." He placed the emphasis on truthful emotions for his actors, which allow the actors to reveal their own style in their stage work. This idea will benefit you when you plan the emotional setting in a truthful mode of thought which will lead to your genuine style of presenting your presentation.

Improving Your Self Image

In the story, "Daddy, I Wanna Be a Salesman," the father told Joey about the importance of liking oneself. What you find and how you feel about what you find is called self image. Did you know that you cannot like anyone more than you like yourself? To be successful in sales, you must like yourself.

R. F. James wrote an interesting article. Here is an excerpt: "Understanding the psychology of the self can mean the difference between success and failure, love and hate, bitterness and happiness. The discovery of the real self can rescue a crumbling marriage, recreate a faltering career, transform victims of 'personality failure.' On another plane, discovering your real self means the difference between freedom and the compulsions of conformity."

It has been proven time and again that a sales person's self image is directly linked to thoughts, which lead to feelings, which then lead to actions that determine the success or failure of a particular endeavor.

In working with sales people who do not have a good self-image, it is important to point out that there is good news. You are not chained and sentenced to life with your self image. You have the wonderful opportunity of changing anything about your attitude which will change your behavior. How you see yourself through your own eyes determines everything else about you and your life. If you don't like yourself, how can anyone else like you? There is enough pressure in the world that is put on us without inflicting additional pressure from ourselves.

Be good to yourself. Treat yourself as you would your best friend by being patient and understanding. When you start making the time to spend with yourself, an interesting thing will begin to happen. You will start to discover different aspects of your inner self that you have overlooked in your daily rush. As you begin to like yourself better, you will treat yourself better. This change in your attitude will lead you to a much more peaceful and rewarding life for you and everyone who has the opportunity of sharing your life.

Using Props in Your Presentation

As in all theater art, props play an intricate role in a stage play. Props are used to communicate, convey, and convince the audience of the author's intent. Your sales presentation should be no different. Have you ever forgotten some important sales tool in your sales presentation? How did you feel when that happened to you? I know a few adjectives to describe the feeling: frustration, anger, and insecurity. To prevent this from occurring, make a list of the necessary props you will need for your presentation; for example:

Crisp, clean copies of your company's applications and forms.
A list of references.
Endorsement letters from satisfied, happy clients.
Articles, summaries, and fact sheets that support your area of persuasion.
Product samples, such as an actual policy.
Product samples, or something tangible that your prospect can touch.
Calculator.
Gold writing pen.
Your company's annual statements, and pictures to familiarize your prospect with your company.
A big sincere smile.

It has been said that a picture is worth a thousand words, and props will multiply that number.

Tips on using props:

Try to get your prospects involved in your presentation, by allowing them to use your props. For instance, if you are working with numbers, let them use your calculator.

In your demonstration, let them scrape the pan, vacuum the rug, push the button or whatever it is that is required to execute the action.

All of the activity should be easy to follow, just as the language you use with your prospect should be.

Do your homework, which means know the why behind your demonstration. Practice performing it, and for your sake, make sure that all the props work prior to performing your presentation.

This is your stage play. Make a powerful impression on your prospect with all of your tools. You have much more control of your presentation than you realize. When you take time to mentally create, physically rehearse, and emotionally believe, your chances of making the sale increase substantially. Remember, don't forget your props.

Stage Fright and Call Reluctance

Actors have all heard of, or experienced, stage fright. In an analysis of this occurrence, we find that it is caused by too much emphasis on one's self. Selling is not excluded from this condition.

In the selling profession, stage fright is referred to as call reluctance. Like stage fright, call reluctance not only hinders your performance, but can eliminate it all together. Many things can cause call reluctance. First, we avoid activities that are unpleasant. Let's face it, no one likes to be rejected or abused, and that is the tape we run in our minds. More times than not, you get what you expect. When you expect to make that appointment, your voice will carry that needed strength to obtain the appointment.

Be Good To Yourself

In selling, you are in charge of yourself, so negotiate. If you know that you need to make 20 calls to get five appointments, in order to make two sales, to earn $1,000 commission, break up the calls. You might just want to make five calls to start. This will lighten your load, and make you feel better. Remember to use your imagination when you have to do something you don't like to do. Act as though you really like doing it. You will find an amazing thing happens. You start to enjoy it. Try it.

Another reason for call reluctance is fear. You may ask yourself, "Am I afraid?" No way. The fact is that no matter who we are, we are all afraid. The fear may not seem apparent, but it exists right below the surface of your consciousness. Fear, many times, will cripple us and prevent us from being human in the sales process. When fear is present, we tend to overcompensate our feelings, and therefore seem fake and insincere to our prospects.

Stanislavski sought to solve the mystery of fear that would sometimes surface in his actors. Sonia Moore wrote in her book, *Stanislavski System*, "Stanislavski saw that, probably because of the artificial atmosphere of the stage in front of a mass of people, an actor's senses often point to paralysis. The actor then loses the feeling of real life and forgets how to do the simplest things that he does naturally and spontaneously in life. Stanislavski realized that an actor has to learn anew to see; and not just to pretend to see to hear, and not just pretend to listen, that he has to talk to his fellow actors and not just to read lines, that he has to think and to feel."

Drive Fear Out

We must learn to relax our bodies, which will relax our minds, and focus not on ourselves and our fears, but on the prospects. When you focus on the prospects, your attention can no longer be on your fears, but rather on their needs and wants. Remember, the mind can hold only one thought at a time, so fill your mind with positive powerful thoughts.

Relaxation

"Therefore, at times of great stress,
it is especially necessary to achieve
a complete freeing of the muscles."

- Constantin Stanislavski

In the business of selling, sales people very rarely take time to relax. In this modern age, many people have forgotten how to relax. However, relaxation is one of the most important parts of effective selling, not to mention effective living.

Stanislavski stressed the role that relaxation plays in acting when he wrote, "What was this quality, common to all great talents? It was easiest of all for me to notice this likeness in their physical freedom, in the lack of all strain. Their bodies were at the call and beck of the inner demands of their wills."

In the studies of the great salespeople of a variety of industries, the findings show that two traits were common among all of them. Those traits were enthusiasm and the ability to be relaxed. When you have control over your body, you are in a better position to control circumstances outside yourself.

The key to realism in acting, as well as in selling, is the ability to perform in a relaxed state of mind with a relaxed body. There are hundreds of things a person can do to relax; from exercising to listening to music, deep breathing, or taking a vacation. In the theater, many actors meditate before rehearsal. Sales people could improve their performance by following the actor's example.

Another great teacher of the theater was Lee Strasberg. In the book, *Strasberg at the Actor Studio*, he discussed some techniques of the art of relaxation that will be a real asset for you. He wrote, "Without relaxation, a lot of things an actor may rightly want to do will be deformed as they enter his instrument, because the instrument itself sets up resistance through tension. When that happens, the actor cannot achieve a real relation between what he is thinking and the expression which should be part of that thought or experience. The expression becomes contaminated."

Stanislavski said, "A lot of actors think they are doing what I recommend but that actually, because of tension, they continue acting as they did before. The actor may think the opposite and even speak of himself as changed, but the impulse, coming into the body, merely takes on the same aspect as before, and can't really quite get through as a fresh impulse and respond." Freeing the body from tension will have a dramatic effect on your sales presentation. Your voice will sound more confident, you will hold yourself better, your eye contact will be more focused, your concentration will be stronger in the execution of your presentation.

Now, for some pointers on relaxation. One exercise used in theater circles is the practice of relaxing your eyelids. Lee Strasberg writes, "Only recently have I realized that this area is involved in life with a great deal of automatic response. On the street, as soon as a particle of dust touches an eyelash, the eyes close. This defensive mechanism is so active and so automatic that a great deal of tension builds up. The tension relaxes simply by permitting the eyelids to droop. As the lids come down, here again you can feel weight actually leaving. Sometimes, when you relax you this area, you get a strange feeling that you are losing control. You have gotten so used to tension as your personal state of equilibrium that when you relax, the muscles momentarily cannot find their own level."

The mind and the body should work as a team. Their actions affect each other. To stimulate one you must, in essence, stimulate the other. To create enthusiasm, many times all that is required is to make a physical movement. For example, clapping your hands will accomplish this. The popular affirmation states, "If you act enthusiastic, you become enthusiastic."

On the other side of the coin, to help your body relax you can create images in your mind which will relax your body. Creative visualization will assist in accomplishing complete relaxation for the body.

In discussing the body and the mind, one must realize that the mind, unlike the body, will not increase production by forcing it, or by trying harder. If you are building a dog house, and you begin hammering the nail into the board, the harder you strike the nail the faster it goes through the board. The mind works exactly opposite of this. The harder you try to think, the less likely you are to get the answer, or to remember something that you are trying to remember. Here is where relaxation can be an ally for you. The prospect is making you rush and is completely controlling the presentation. You find yourself becoming tense. The blood that would reach your brain to assist you in all the thoughts necessary for your presentation has been transferred to the shoulders because you tensed them as a result of stress. This undermines your efforts and puts you at a disadvantage in dealing with your prospects.

You are now in another encounter with your prospect. However, this time you are relaxed. The prospect makes objections which you calmly overcome with the correct response simply because you are relaxed. The relaxed mind can think and can respond better without the tension that distracts and impairs the thought process. Learn to relax and discover the hidden power of your personality just below the surface.

Stanislavski wrote, "It can be compared to the feelings of a prisoner when the chains that had interfered with all his movements for years have at last been removed. I luxuriated in this condition on the stage, sincerely believing that in it lay the whole secret, the whole soul of creativeness on the stage, that all the rest would come from this state and perception of physical freedom. Thoughts are embodied in acts. And a man's actions, in turn, affect his mind. His mind affects his body and again, his body, or its condition, and its reflex action on his mind produces this or that condition." You must learn how to rest your body, free your muscles and at the same time, your psyche.

Director

"Directing is a precise science not vague thought and fantasy"
- Constantin Stanislavski

A director is responsible for the overall outcome of a play's production. He is in charge of seeing that the set is built and the actors are able to perform their roles effectively. The director has blocked the movement of the actors and has used all the space available on stage. He has studied the script and has a deep understanding of the author's intent, which he expresses through the actors and the given circumstances. He brings life to the words and makes it all happen. The director in the theater is a leader, not a manager. Sales managers would do well to change their titles to sales leaders. There was an interesting message from the Wall Street Journal that read,

> "People don't want to be managed, they want to be lead. Who ever heard of a world manager? World leader, yes. Educational leader. Political leader. Scout leader. Community leader. Labor leader. Business leader. They lead. They don't manage. The carrot always wins over the stick. Ask your horse. You can lead your horse to water, but you can't manage him to drink. If you want to manage somebody, manage yourself. Do that well and you'll be ready to stop managing. And start leading."

In the business world, the sales leader/manager is, in a sense, the director. The sales quotes fall on his shoulders. The success of the company is his responsibility. He is in charge of the office, as well as the dress code of the sales profession. He has had the sales people trained and has helped them develop their roles. He has studied the product and has a deep understanding of the product knowledge. He has a mental grasp of the goals and objectives of his company. He brings sales figures to life, and he makes it happen. He does it through his people.

It has been said that morale filters down from the top. In the sales office, that couldn't be more true. The tempo-rhythm of the office is determined by the sales manager's attitude.

Vladimir I. Nemirovich-Danchenko is quoted as saying, "The director must die within an actor." In the world of selling, it could be said that the sales manager should be reflected in his sales people. Imitation is the greatest form of flattery. Sales professionals should have their own style; however, it is necessary to have a role model from which to pattern their style. Stanislavski said that, "Directing is a precise science, not vague thoughts and fantasy."

There should be no guesswork in sales management. Sonia Moore, in her book entitled, *The Stanislavski System*, writes that, "The director must have imagination and be capable of invention; he must have culture, taste, tact and principles. A director sometimes tries too hard to establish his own prestige. He has no right to distort the idea of the author for the sake of his own intentions. But, he has a right to insist on the realization of his ideas."

Sales experience will make the sales manager more empathetic toward his staff. He should always build his staff's esteem. This is done through encouragement, recognition of accomplishments, and time. Time spent listening to the sales professional is an investment that will return your investment tenfold. Sonia Moore, in the discussion of directing said, "The director must sense an actor's individuality and be able to create the whole with various individualities. This, however, does not mean that he should adapt himself to an actor. The director should not demand the same colors from different actors. Neither should he demand definite results, a definite expression for gesture or intonation, at the very start.

Rehearsals will proceed well after the director's ideas have reached the actors. This will be achieved through discussion, when he checks his ideas with the group."

As in the theater, the sales director should work with his people in a similar fashion. Group discussions are a powerful way for the sales people to voice their victories, as well as talk about their setbacks, and can give others a chance to share some helpful ideas with that person.

The 80-20 formula applies in most areas of life, especially in the business of selling. Eighty percent of the sales in the company comes from 20 percent of the sales professionals. With the Method Selling training program, the sales professional stands a better chance of not just staying in the business, but making the job more enjoyable, which will result in more money. The sales director is the coach, the builder of the team. It is a big responsibility; however, it is so satisfying, watching your staff grow from shy introverted rookies to dynamic articulate sales professionals.

Conclusion

Method Selling is built on the premise that all the elements are working together to produce the full power of the system. Let us walk through the Method Selling system.

The initial step for you is to focus on your Super Objective. Mentally create a picture of the role you play, followed by deep breathing coupled with muscle relaxation.

The "Given Circumstances," in this case, are the situation, the location, prospect, and sales material.

You can now use the "Magic If" to stimulate your inner feelings of creativity. You would think, "What if this person were an old friend from childhood? How would I greet him?"

The next step is awakening the "Imagination," which can mentally recreate the scenes necessary to provide you with the stimulation to create your role. Your experience was reinforced by the emotion that was tied to it in its initial stage.

By reconstructing the "Emotional Memory," you will be more believable to the prospect. You will tap into a past experience, which will move your emotional state to reflect the emotion needed in your presentation.

You must focus your attention on the scene and the prospect in the "Concentration of Attention." Your thoughts must be honed in on all of the events taking place in the sales situation. You must be centered in your presentation with your prospect which will create an irresistible atmosphere of warmth and love.

You must, once in the sales situation, create affinity by "Adaptation" with the prospect. This encompasses verbal, social, and posture affinity.

In presenting your sales presentation, you must "Communicate" with the prospect in a warm, friendly, persuasive manner, as well as perform it on the prospect's "sense speech" level.

You must conduct your "Tempo-rhythm" in such a way as to match the motion of your prospects, which is necessary to successfully close the sale.

The foundation of the sales presentation was built on the "Truth and Belief" element. The truth is, the product that you are marketing is a benefit, and will do all the things that it claims to do; that you wholeheartedly believe in the company, the product, and yourself. You are also committed to meeting the needs of your prospects and you care for them; a simplified view of Method Selling in a nutshell.

From the results of research and insight into the selling world, it is apparent that Method Selling will enhance and sharpen any sales person's skill in the art of professional selling. The information on capitalism helped reinforce the belief that salesmanship is possible because of this economic system. The comparison with communism furthers the understanding of the benefit of this great economic system.

The comic book entitled, "Daddy, I Wanna Be A Salesman," shared some valuable advice to the sales person. Looking at selling through the eyes of children provided a deeper understanding into the world of professional selling. The chapter on the elements of persuasion was instrumental in the development of a heightened awareness in fully understanding persuasion.

The main part of the project in the Method Selling program, based on the teaching of Constantin Stanislavski and his lifetime work on the Method of Physical Action, provided the framework on which the Method Selling project was written. Stanislavski's teachings have been recognized worldwide as a method to effectively train actors to become much more believable and dynamic in the roles they play on stage. Those same principles have been organized and adapted to apply to the sales professional. The insights into the physical movement and elements of physical action are invaluable when discussing human engineering and performance.

Method Selling will assist you in personalizing your role as a sales professional. I challenge you to study the concepts presented in the book. You will find that Stanislavski made a tremendous contribution into the lives of thousands of actors. You are the beneficiary of this remarkable man's lifetime work in discovering the path to your optimum performance in the role you play in this life.

Bibliography

Allen, Charles, *You Are Not Alone*, Carmen, NY, 1978, pg. 19, 112, 115.

Barker, Larry, *Communications*, Santa Monica, CA, 1963, pg. 64.

Bunting, John R., *Hidden Face of Free Enterprise*, McGraw-Hill, 1964, pg. 23.

Carnegie, Dale, *How to Win Friends and Influence People*, Simon and Schuster, New York, NY, 1936, pg. 118, 121.

Covey, Stephen R., *The 7 Habits of Highly Effective People*, Simon and Schuster, New York, NY, 1988, pg.127, 131.

Dimnet, Ernest, *The Art of Thinking*, Simon and Schuster, New York, NY, 1928, pg. 57.

Doss, Richard, *Theory P*, Human Side Press, Houston, TX, 1992, pg. 47

Fatjo, Tom, *With No Fear of Failure*, Word Books, Waco, TX, 1981, pg. 31.

Fisher, Roger and Ury, William, *Getting to Yes*, Penguin Group, New York, NY, 1981, pg. 126, 127.

Galbraith, John Kenneth, *American Capitalism*, Riverside Press, Cambridge, MA, 1952, pg. 22.

Gorchakov, Nikolai A., *The Theater in Soviet Russia*, Columbia Press, New York, NY, 1957, pg. 1, 46, 47, 61.

Heilbroner, Robert L., *Limits of American Capitalism*, Harper & Row Publishers, New York, NY, pg. 22.

Hill, Napoleon, *Think and Grow Rich*, Fawcett Crest Publications, New York, NY, 1960, pg. 42, 56.

Hobbes, Thomas, *Founders of American Economic Thought*, Bookman & Assoc., 1958, New York, NY, pg. 33, 34.

Insight, September 1989 issue, Nightingale-Conant Corp., Chicago, IL, pg. 65

Mandino, Og, *The Greatest Salesman in the World*, Frederick Fell, New York, NY, 1972, pg. 50, 120.

Marx, Karl and Engle, Frederick, *The Communist Manifesto*, Modern Reader Paperback, NY, 1962, pg. 22.

Meyers, Paul, *The Dynamics of Goal Setting*, Success Motivational Institute, 1960, pg. 9, 28, 29.

Molloy, John T., *How to Work the Competition into the Ground & Have Fun Doing It*, Warner Books, New York, NY, 1987, pg. 55

Moore, Sonia, *The Stanislavski System*, The Viking Press, New York, NY, 1974, pg. 25, 50, 54, 59, 65, 80, 141, 148.

Peale, Norman Vincent, *The Tough Minded Optimist*, Fawcett Crest Books Publication, 1961, Greenwich, CN, pg. viii, 75.

Rand, Ayn, *Capitalism, the Unknown Ideal*, American Library, Inc., New York, NY, 1962, pg. 18, 19.

Shaftebury, Edmund, *Mental Magnetism*, Ralston University Press, Meriden, CT, 1925, pg. 76.

Smith, Adam, *Knowledge Products*, P.O. Box 00340, Nashville, TN, pg. 20, 23.

Sound Selling - The Audio Magazine for Sales Success, Vol. 10, Nightingale-Conant Corp., Chicago, IL, pg. 61.

Stanislavski, Constantin, *An Actor's Handbook*, Theater Arts Books, New York, NY, 1963, pg. 25, 31, 37, 38, 46, 57, 60, 64.

Stanislavski, Constantin, *My Life in Art*, Theater Arts Books, New York, NY, 1948, pg. 12, 15, 18, 27, 38, 39, 43, 45, 46, 48, 53, 70 71, 75, 111, 143, 144.

Strasberg, Lee, *Strasberg at the Actor's Studio*, Viking Press, New York, NY, 1965, pg. 18, 54, 58, 143, 144.

Webster's New World Dictionary, 2nd College Ed., William Collins+World Publishing Co., Inc., 1974, pg. 21, 122, 126.

Weed, Joseph, *Psychic Energy*, Parker Publications, West Myech, NJ, pg. 50.

Wolfe, Vernon V., *Unfolding Potential*, Provo, Utah, pg. 49, 51.

Subject Index

QUESTIONNAIRE

1. How long have you been in the sales profession? ______________

2. How many sales books do you read each year?________________
3. What type of industry are you currently working in for your career?____

4. What is your age?_______________________________________

5. What is your gender?_____________________________________

6. What is your nationality?_________________________________
7. What do you like best about *The Magic of Method Selling*?_______ ____

8. Do you listen to audio cassettes for self development and learning? ____

9. Would you like to receive our newsletter?____________________

10. Would you be interested in attending a seminar on Method Selling? ____

We value your feedback, so take just a few minutes and share with us your feelings as they pertain to *The Magic of Method Selling*.

____

____

____

____

ORDER FORM

For additional copies please, fill out the order form.

NAME:____

COMPANY:______________________________________

ADDRESS:______________________________________

PHONE NUMBER:__________________________________

CITY, STATE, ZIP:_________________________________

NUMBER OF COPIES:__________________

A special 10% discount applies to orders over 50 copies. In addition, if you are ordering 200 copies or more you may deduct 15%. Please allow two weeks for delivery. Remember to add your state sales tax and just $2 for shipping and handling. Send in your questionnaire for your special gift.

Mail to:

> Cut to the Chase Publications
> 113191 Westheimer, Suite 385
> Houston, Texas 77042

COMING ATTRACTIONS:
Living the Magic of Method Selling (Fall, 97)

James M. Rankin

ABOUT THE AUTHOR

James M. Rankin is president of Rankin Marketing and Communications located in Houston, Texas. He is a graduate of Southwest Texas State University and went on to earn his Masters in Business Administration along with his Doctorate of Philosophy in Business Administration from Kennedy Western University. He has published numerous articles on sales, marketing, motivation, including a short story.

James was selected as one of the Outstanding Young Men in America in 1985. He is field tested and a seasoned professional in the insurance, investment field. First, as a leading producer for a National company, as well as having served as a District Manager. He was one of the youngest Regional Directors in the industry. He has recruited and trained more than 100 producers. As a District Manager, he guided his agency to annual sales of over 12 million dollars in production. He has also built several multi-million dollar sales organizations.

As an actor, he starred as Tom Sawyer and has appeared in numerous plays such as Our Town, My Fair Lady, Member of the Wedding, and Showboat. He has also directed several plays. Moreover, he has also published numerous play critiques for a newspaper and magazine. In addition, James has written and directed a radio theater production entitled, Divine Deformity, and has hosted numerous radio prograrns.

James is a dynamic speaker and sales trainer. He has been featured in Nightingale Conant Sound Selling Program. He is single and resides in Houston, Texas.